Ritalin and Other Methylphenidate-Containing Drugs

DRUGS The Straight Facts

Alcohol

Antidepressants

Body Enhancement Products

Cocaine

Date Rape Drugs

Designer Drugs

Diet Pills

Ecstasy

Hallucinogens

Heroin

Inhalants

Marijuana

Nicotine

Prescription Pain Relievers

Ritalin and Other Methylphenidate-Containing Drugs

Sleep Aids

■ DRUGS
The Straight Facts

Ritalin and Other Methylphenidate-Containing Drugs

Carmen Ferreiro

Consulting Editor

David J. Triggle

University Professor
School of Pharmacy and Pharmaceutical Sciences
State University of New York at Buffalo

CHELSEA HOUSE
P U B L I S H E R S
A Haights Cross Communications Company
Philadelphia

CHELSEA HOUSE PUBLISHERS
VP, NEW PRODUCT DEVELOPMENT Sally Cheney
DIRECTOR OF PRODUCTION Kim Shinners
CREATIVE MANAGER Takeshi Takahashi
MANUFACTURING MANAGER Diann Grasse

Staff for RITALIN AND OTHER METHYLPHENIDATE-CONTAINING DRUGS
EXECUTIVE EDITOR Tara Koellhoffer
ASSOCIATE EDITOR Beth Reger
PRODUCTION EDITOR Noelle Nardone
ASSOCIATE PHOTO EDITOR Noelle Nardone
SERIES & COVER DESIGNER Terry Mallon
LAYOUT 21st Century Publishing and Communications, Inc.

A Haights Cross Communications ✦ Company

http://www.chelseahouse.com

First Printing

1 3 5 7 9 8 6 4 2

Library of Congress Cataloging-in-Publication Data

Ferreiro, Carmen.
  Ritalin and other methylphenidate-containing drugs / Carmen Ferreiro.
    p. cm.—(Drugs, the straight facts)
  Includes bibliographical references and index.
  ISBN 0-7910-7637-7 (1)
  1. Methylphenidate hydrochloride. 2. Attention-deficit hyperactivity disorder.
I. Title. II. Series.
RJ506.H9F47 2004
618.92'8589061—dc22

                                      2004010504

All links and web addresses were checked and verified to be correct at the time
of publication. Because of the dynamic nature of the web, some addresses and
links may have changed since publication and may no longer be valid.

Table of Contents

The Use and Abuse of Drugs

The issues associated with drug use and abuse in contemporary society are vexing subjects, fraught with political agendas and ideals that often obscure essential information that teens need to know to have intelligent discussions about how to best deal with the problems associated with drug use and abuse. *Drugs: The Straight Facts* aims to provide this essential information through straightforward explanations of how an individual drug or group of drugs works in both therapeutic and non-therapeutic conditions; with historical information about the use and abuse of specific drugs; with discussion of drug policies in the United States; and with an ample list of further reading.

From the start, the series uses the word *"drug"* to describe psychoactive substances that are used for medicinal or non-medicinal purposes. Included in this broad category are substances that are legal or illegal. It is worth noting that humans have used many of these substances for hundreds, if not thousands, of years. For example, traces of marijuana and cocaine have been found in Egyptian mummies; the use of peyote and Amanita fungi has long been a component of religious ceremonies worldwide; and alcohol production and consumption have been an integral part of many human cultures' social and religious ceremonies. One can speculate about why early human societies chose to use such drugs. Perhaps, anything that could provide relief from the harshness of life—anything that could make the poor conditions and fatigue associated with hard work easier to bear—was considered a welcome tonic. Life was likely to be, according to the seventeenth century English philosopher Thomas Hobbes, *"poor, nasty, brutish and short."* One can also speculate about modern human societies' continued use and abuse of drugs. Whatever the reasons, the consequences of sustained drug use are not insignificant—addiction, overdose, incarceration, and drug wars—and must be dealt with by an informed citizenry.

The problem that faces our society today is how to break

the connection between our demand for drugs and the willingness of largely outside countries to supply this highly profitable trade. This is the same problem we have faced since narcotics and cocaine were outlawed by the Harrison Narcotic Act of 1914, and we have yet to defeat it despite current expenditures of approximately $20 billion per year on "the war on drugs." The first step in meeting any challenge is always an intelligent and informed citizenry. The purpose of this series is to educate our readers so that they can make informed decisions about issues related to drugs and drug abuse.

SUGGESTED ADDITIONAL READING

David T. Courtwright, *Forces of Habit. Drugs and the Making of the Modern World.* Cambridge, Mass.: Harvard University Press, 2001. David Courtwright is Professor of History at the University of North Florida.

Richard Davenport-Hines, *The Pursuit of Oblivion. A Global History of Narcotics.* New York: Norton, 2002. The author is a professional historian and a member of the Royal Historical Society.

Aldous Huxley, *Brave New World.* New York: Harper & Row, 1932. Huxley's book, written in 1932, paints a picture of a cloned society devoted only to the pursuit of happiness.

David J. Triggle, Ph.D.
University Professor
School of Pharmacy and Pharmaceutical Sciences
State University of New York at Buffalo

1

Methylphenidate: Miracle Pill or Legal Speed?

WHAT IS METHYLPHENIDATE?

Methylphenidate (e.g., Ritalin® and Concerta®) is a stimulant drug prescribed to treat hyperactivity, impulsivity, and inattention in millions of American children. Methylphenidate was first synthesized in the mid-1940s in Europe. In the United States, it was approved by the Food and Drug Administration (FDA) in 1955. The effects of methylphenidate in the human body are almost identical to those of the amphetamines. Amphetamines—the collective name for levoamphetamine (Benzedrine), dextroamphetamine (Dexedrine®), and methamphetamine (Methedrine or "speed")—are known to be potent psychomotor stimulants.

Because of methylphenidate's potential risk for addiction and abuse, the U.S. Drug Enforcement Administration (DEA) classifies it in the Schedule II category of drugs, which includes cocaine, opium, morphine, and other narcotics, and barbiturates—all drugs that carry a significant risk of abuse. To be included in the Schedule II category means the DEA must approve how much of the drug can be produced yearly.

Schedule I, a more restrictive category, includes drugs such as

Table 1.1 Examples of Drugs in the Five Scheduling Categories

Schedule I	Ecstasy, China White, GHB, Heroin (synthetic and natural), Lysergic Acid Diethylamide (LSD), Marijuana, Mescaline, Peyote, Psilocin and Psilocybin (constituents of magic mushrooms)
Schedule II	Amphetamine, Cocaine and Crack, Codeine, Fentanyl, Hydrocodone, Meperidine (Demerol®), Methadone, Methylphenidate (Ritalin), Morphine, Opium, Oxycodone (OxyContin®, Percocet®), Phencyclidine (PCP)
Schedule III	Anabolic steroids, Barbiturates, Ketamine, LSD precursors
Schedule IV	Alprazolam (Xanax®), Clonazepam (Klonopin®, Clonopin®), Diazepam (Valium®), Flunitrazepam (Rohypnol), Lorazepam (Ativan®), Triazolam (Halcion®), Zolpidem (Ambien®)
Schedule V	Codeine preparations—200 mg/ml or 100 g (Cosanyl, Robitussin A-C®, Cheracol®, Cerose®, Pedciacof®)

heroin and LSD that are considered to have no recognized medical purpose and are illegal in the United States, outside of FDA-approved research (Table 1.1).

Methylphenidate is both a legal drug, when taken under medical prescription, and an illegal one, when used for recreational purposes. It is also the only Schedule II substance whose legal production has increased in the last decade. In 1997, the production quota for methylphenidate authorized by the DEA was 13,824 kg—a 700% increase from the 1990 quota. This increase has come at the request of the pharmaceutical companies that manufacture the drug, which say they cannot keep up with the demand from doctors' prescriptions. More than 90% of methylphenidate is prescribed for children.

These numbers make some experts uneasy, because, like Sydney Walker III (psychiatrist and author of *The Hyperactivity Hoax*), they believe that Ritalin is "a powerful and potentially addictive drug that masks symptoms without treating the disease and whose long-term effects on the brain are completely unknown."[1] Others, on the contrary, consider methylphenidate a mild stimulant that calms children and helps them concentrate.

Because of these opposing viewpoints, the medical use of Ritalin has become quite controversial. Many books and articles have been published on the subject, raising the public's awareness about the drug and its effects, and leaving many to wonder whether Ritalin is a miracle pill that solves a medical problem or a way of drugging children into being more compliant and easy to handle.

HUMANS AND STIMULANTS THROUGH HISTORY: A LOVE AFFAIR

The use of stimulants for medical purposes has a long history. People have chewed on plant products such as coca and tobacco leaves for centuries to relieve pain and enhance feelings of well-being. When cocaine, the active ingredient of coca, was extracted from the plant in the late 19th century, it was prescribed specifically for its stimulating properties to treat everything from depression to rheumatism. Amphetamines, synthesized at about the same time, were embraced by the medical community for their mood-elevating effects. For some time, amphetamines were prescribed for many diverse conditions, such as schizophrenia, heart problems, infantile cerebral palsy, seasickness, and persistent hiccups, simply because they made patients feel better.

This effect is not surprising: Amphetamines are potent psychomotor stimulants. Whether sniffed, swallowed, snorted, or injected, they induce feelings of power, strength, exhilaration, self-assertion, focus, and enhanced motivation. Amphetamine intake causes a release of the excitatory neurotransmitters dopamine and noradrenaline (norepinephrine) in the central nervous system (CNS). The release of dopamine typically induces a sense of aroused euphoria that may last several hours; unlike cocaine, amphetamine is not readily broken down by the body. After taking amphetamines, feelings are intensified, the need to sleep or eat is diminished, and the user may feel as though he or she can "take on the world."

Amphetamines not only improve vigilance and accuracy in performing tasks, but they also improve the individual's attitude about doing work, especially when the required tasks are repetitive and boring. The euphoria does not last, however, and is followed by an intense mental depression and fatigue as the amphetamines deplete the neuronal stores of dopamine in the limbic system, the pleasure center of the brain (see Chapter 3).

In the short term, the only negative effects of taking amphetamines are insomnia, or inability to sleep, and loss of appetite. In the long run, however, the negative effects of the drugs become more apparent. Amphetamines are addictive, which means the user can become dependent on them. Over time, too, the user builds up a tolerance to the drug and needs larger and larger doses to obtain the same effect.

Methylphenidate was synthesized in 1944 in Europe in an unsuccessful attempt to create a stimulant that would not produce addiction or tolerance (Figure 1.1). Introduced in the United States in 1955, it was first approved by the FDA for the treatment of drug-induced lethargy, mild depression, and narcolepsy. In the early 1960s, the drug was first marketed under the name Ritalin to improve memory in elderly patients and to treat several behavioral problems in children.

STIMULANTS AND CHILD BEHAVIOR: THE PARADOXICAL EFFECT

The effect of stimulants on child behavior was first reported in 1937. Charles Bradley, a physician working with children of normal intelligence who had neurological and behavioral disorders, prescribed Benzedrine to treat headaches in children who had undergone a spinal tap. Although the headaches did not disappear with the amphetamines, the children's level of activity decreased tremendously and their academic performance and compliance increased.

Bradley was puzzled by his finding. "It appears paradoxical," he wrote, "that a drug known to be a stimulant should produce subdued behavior."[2] To explain this result, he proposed that the amphetamines were, in fact, stimulating a hypothetical center in the brain that was responsible for inhibiting activity. Although his theory turned out to be wrong, many doctors and parents still believe in his notion that Ritalin and other amphetamines, when given in low doses, help calm hyperactive children. This effect, they believe, is distinct from the stimulating properties that amphetamines have on healthy children or adults.

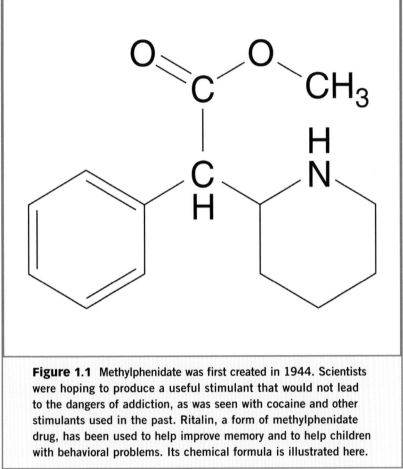

Figure 1.1 Methylphenidate was first created in 1944. Scientists were hoping to produce a useful stimulant that would not lead to the dangers of addiction, as was seen with cocaine and other stimulants used in the past. Ritalin, a form of methylphenidate drug, has been used to help improve memory and to help children with behavioral problems. Its chemical formula is illustrated here.

The first experiment to disprove Bradley's theory of the "paradoxical" or reverse effect was conducted in 1980 by Judy Rapoport and her colleagues at the National Institute of Mental Health (NIMH). Under well-controlled conditions, they surveyed the cognitive and behavioral effects of stimulants on both hyperactive and non-hyperactive children. Their results showed that both groups performed better when taking stimulants. In other words, the researchers found that stimulants have the same effect on children whether they are hyperactive or normal. Thus, there is no paradoxical effect.

That stimulants should increase children's performance is not surprising when we consider that stimulants have the same effect on adults. From the caffeine in the coffee adults drink when they feel drowsy to the over-the-counter "pep pills" college students take to help them study late into the night, stimulants help individuals be more alert, concentrate better, and think more clearly. These effects, however, do not last indefinitely. Also, when taken in excess, stimulants actually make the user feel drugged and sluggish. As with any drug, there is no way to predict when this will happen.

On the other hand, the idea that stimulants *calm* hyperactive children seems to go against logic. How can a stimulant calm someone down? In fact, stimulants do not calm children, at least not directly. They do, however, increase children's concentration and their level of interest. As a consequence of these effects, the children seem less active because they are more focused on what they are learning or doing.

To understand this, let's imagine that you are listening to a lecture. If you are not interested in the subject, you may become bored and start to fidget. But if you took a stimulant such as Ritalin before attending the lecture, you would find the lecture more interesting and may not fidget as much. An observer, who only sees your behavior, might come to the conclusion that your level activity has been directly decreased by the stimulant.

THE RISE OF RITALIN

During the 1940s and 1950s, Charles Bradley continued to publish anecdotal evidence that amphetamines helped children's performance. Only in the early 1960s, when several clinical trials showed the effectiveness of Ritalin and a similar drug, Dexedrine, and the FDA approved Ritalin to treat various behavioral problems in children, did the use of Ritalin increase noticeably.

Ritalin became popular primarily because it was *not* an amphetamine. Amphetamines were known to have the potential for abuse and addiction. The potential for abuse of and addiction to Ritalin was still unknown. Ritalin was also preferred because it had been shown in many studies to have a rapid positive effect on children's performance, it remained in the bloodstream for only a few hours, and it had no negative effect after the children stopped taking the drug.

In the 1960s, Ritalin was prescribed for children identified as having personality-driven symptoms—the condition first called MBD (minimal brain dysfunction) and hyperkinetic reaction. Having "excessive motor activity" was a prerequisite to fit into this category. As a result, many children were not considered eligible for Ritalin.

By 1970, only about 150,000 children were taking Ritalin. During the 1970s, the central problem of the condition was redefined as one of poor attention and distractibility with no mention of hyperactivity. In 1980, psychiatrists' official guidelines on defining the condition were revised, and attention-deficit/hyperactivity disorder (ADHD), was added as a new disease. Millions of children who were not hyperactive fit the description of this new disease and could be prescribed Ritalin for their symptoms. Not surprisingly, the number of elementary school children taking Ritalin increased, from 270,000 to 541,000 in 1980 to 750,000 in 1987.[3]

The DEA production quota, which was a steady annual output of approximately 1,700 kg through the 1980s, started to

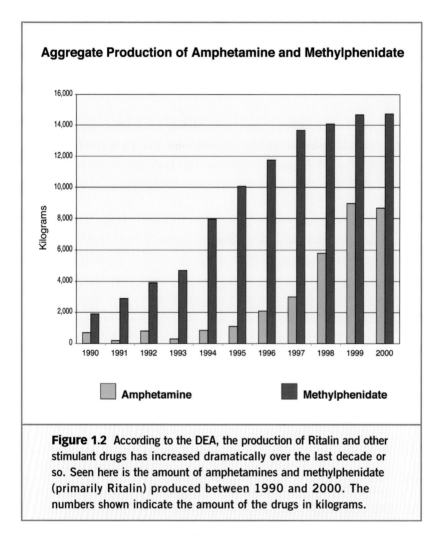

Aggregate Production of Amphetamine and Methylphenidate

Kilograms

□ Amphetamine   ■ Methylphenidate

Figure 1.2 According to the DEA, the production of Ritalin and other stimulant drugs has increased dramatically over the last decade or so. Seen here is the amount of amphetamines and methylphenidate (primarily Ritalin) produced between 1990 and 2000. The numbers shown indicate the amount of the drugs in kilograms.

increase dramatically each year, beginning in 1991 (Figure 1.2). In 1993, the quota was 5,110 kg; in 1996, it was 11,775 kg. Although some Ritalin is used to treat resistant depression and the mental and neurological deterioration associated with AIDS, most is used to treat ADHD.

The rise in the production of Ritalin paralleled an increase in the media's coverage of ADHD. Television talk shows, newspapers, and magazine articles began to alert parents to this new disorder that might be affecting their children and its supposed "cure." ADHD and Ritalin made the cover of *Time* magazine in 1994; at about the same time, the book *Driven to Distraction: Recognizing and Coping with Attention Deficit Disorder from Childhood Through Adulthood*, by Edward Hallowell and John Ratey, was climbing the best-seller list. Until then, ADHD had been considered solely a childhood disease. In this book, Hallowell and Ratey argued that ADHD affects adults, too. In fact, they both claimed to have ADHD and to be taking Ritalin. An increase in the numbers of adults taking Ritalin followed these revelations.

THE EFFECTS OF RITALIN AS A LEGAL DRUG

Today, in the United States, Ritalin is available by prescription as a small yellow or white pill. The recommended starting dosage is 5 milligrams once a day, usually at breakfast. To find the optimal dose, the dosage is increased by increments of 2.5 milligrams, and a second dose at noon, or even a third dose, is added until behavioral symptoms improve. Ritalin's effects begin within 30 to 60 minutes of taking the medication, they peak within 1 to 3 hours, and they disappear after 3 to 5 hours. Within 12 to 24 hours, the drug has been totally metabolized by the body and is out of the system.

There are also sustained-release forms of methylphenidate. The effects of Ritalin SR® (sustained release) last from 4 to 6 hours. A newer formulation called Concerta™, which arrived on the market in 2002, lasts up to 12 hours and needs to be taken only once daily.

The short-term positive effects of Ritalin on children's behavior have been reported by parents and teachers. According to Lawrence H. Diller in his book *Running on Ritalin*, "Between 60 and 90 percent of children with attention, behavioral, or school performance problems improve at least somewhat when taking Ritalin."[4]

The two most common side effects of Ritalin are insomnia and loss of appetite, both of which are known side effects of all stimulants. In a report on ADHD that aired in 1995 on PBS, a child explained how he felt after taking Ritalin: "You are tired but you can't sleep. Tired with hyperness . . . and you can't sleep because your mind is still awake."[5] His words echoed the experience of cocaine users

HYPERACTIVITY

After Andrew got in trouble for the third time in a week for interrupting his class, his first-grade teacher asked his parents to attend a meeting to discuss Andrew's behavior. Andrew's father was angry. His son was perfectly behaved at home. He thought it was the teacher's fault that Andrew misbehaved. Andrew's mother, however, was not so sure. Andrew seemed to get into fights when playing with other children, and doing homework was a struggle for him. He completed his math homework quickly while standing by his chair and singing the numbers. However, he took a long time to write a list of words and color a picture. Many times, Andrew forgot to bring his homework to school. He never put it back in his backpack. His mother had given up asking him to do it, and just packed it herself.

"But," the father insisted, "except for homework, we have no problems with him."

"What about meals?" the teacher asked.

The father shrugged. "He likes to run around, so we don't make him sit with us."

who cannot sleep because they cannot stop their wired brains from racing.

The loss of appetite some users experience does not necessarily translate into stunted growth. Usually, a growth rebound occurs after the first year of treatment and during periods when children are not taking the medication, such as weekends and holidays.

According to the *Physician's Desk Reference* (PDR), the manual provided by drug manufacturers, other adverse

---

"And shopping? Does he behave when you are at the mall?"

"We never take him."

"He used to run away and get lost," his mother added. "We don't take him anymore. It is not safe."

By the end of the meeting, Andrew's father reluctantly admitted that maybe Andrew's problems were not only happening at school. When the teacher suggested that Andrew might benefit from Ritalin, his parents agreed to give it a try.

While taking Ritalin, Andrew's behavior improved. He did not fidget as much and listened to the teacher without interrupting. However, he still needed extra attention from her. The parents asked for special arrangements, and an extra helper was assigned to help Andrew stay on task. Eventually, the medication was discontinued, but his workload was altered to include modified spelling lists and shorter writing assignments.

For Andrew, as for many hyperactive children, receiving one-on-one attention made a great difference.

reactions to Ritalin include nervousness, rashes, anorexia, nausea, dizziness, headaches, cardiac arrhythmia, blood pressure changes, angina, abdominal pain, weight loss, and, in rare cases, anemia, transient depression, and hair loss.

One to 10% of the children who take Ritalin develop involuntary movements, or tics, such as blinking, playing with their fingers, or shoulder shrugging. These symptoms are usually associated with dyskinesias (abnormal muscle movements that stem from disrupted brain function), and also with Tourette's syndrome (a condition in which the tics are accompanied by uncontrollable vocalization of one or more words or sounds, which are often offensive). Although there was some preliminary evidence that Ritalin caused liver cancer in rats, further research did not substantiate this finding in humans.

Ritalin may also have negative effects on behavior. About 30% of the children taking Ritalin experience a rebound effect—that is, they experience a time, often in the late afternoon, during which they are irritable and reactive. Usually, if the child takes a smaller dose of Ritalin in the afternoon, the symptoms of the rebound effect will be reduced without any substantial change in the appetite or sleep patterns.

Some experts have reported that children taking Ritalin experience a change in the cognitive and intellectual processes. Parents and teachers have noticed that some children answer questions in more compliant or narrow ways, which could suggest that their creative thinking is restricted. The results of the studies on these effects are not consistent. In some cases, children on Ritalin become withdrawn, too focused, zombie-like, somber, and quiet, and spend increasing amounts of time alone. Ritalin can also cause "toxic psychosis," a syndrome that includes symptoms of hallucinations, delirium, and sometimes violent behavior. Usually, this occurs with an overdose, but it has sometimes been reported with standard doses.

The long-term effects of Ritalin are not clear. It is known that Ritalin does not cure ADHD, but merely reduces the symptoms of hyperactivity, poor attention, and impulsivity. When the patient stops taking Ritalin, no matter how long he or she has been taking it, the effects of the medication will disappear.

2

Ritalin and Attention-Deficit/ Hyperactivity Disorder

WHAT IS ATTENTION-DEFICIT/HYPERACTIVITY DISORDER?

About 3.5 million Americans, most of them children, have been diagnosed with attention-deficit/hyperactivity disorder (ADHD) and prescribed Ritalin or a similar drug to offset their symptoms. Despite these numbers, many people believe that ADHD does not exist. In a sense, whether ADHD exists or not is basically a matter of semantics, a disagreement over what the term *ADHD* means. No one would contend that some children do have problems paying attention, lack self-control, and are hyperactive to such an extreme that they cannot perform well in an academic or social environment. In the American Psychiatric Association's *Diagnostic and Statistical Manual of Mental Disorders (DSM)*, ADHD is defined as lack of concentration, poor self-control, and/or hyperactivity. Using this definition, ADHD clearly exists. On the other hand, some professionals argue that to give these symptoms a name and list them in a book as a diagnosis is misleading, because ADHD is not a disease or a diagnosis, but only a list of symptoms with many possible causes.

Sydney Walker III illustrates the difference between a symptom and a diagnosis in the following example from his book *The Hyperactivity Hoax*:

> Let's say you come down with a chronic cough. Should your doctor say, "You have a coughing disorder," and prescribe cough drops—without worrying about whether you have lung cancer, strep throat, or tuberculosis? Or if you develop a swollen leg, should you doctor diagnose it as a "lump," and give you an aspirin, without determining whether that lump is a tumor, an insect bite, or gangrene?[6]

Coughing or swollen legs are symptoms, not diseases in themselves. In this sense, ADHD is not a disease either. In the opinion of Walker and others, to say that a child has ADHD does not explain the underlying cause of the hyperactivity or lack of concentration. To them, giving a name to the condition may hide the fact that not much is known about what is wrong with the affected individual and may inhibit people from looking for the cause that would lead to a more permanent solution.

Regarding the treatment for ADHD, few will argue that the short-term effects of Ritalin on some children with ADHD are impressive. Yet not even the staunchest advocates of Ritalin will claim that it "cures" ADHD. On the contrary, the fact that the child seems to do better while taking Ritalin may give parents and physicians the false impression that the problem is solved and, as a consequence, prevent them from doing anything else to address the problem.

ADHD: A HISTORY

Although the term *attention deficit disorder (ADD)*, as ADHD was first called when the condition was named, had been in use since the 1970s, the problem was not new. There have always been children who were more active, distractible, and impulsive than others.

Historically, the first cases of children with ADHD were presented by the British physician George Still (Figure 2.1) in 1902 during a lecture to the Royal College of Medicine. Still described a group of 20 children as being aggressive, defiant, resistant to discipline, and excessively emotional or passionate. In a note that paralleled modern ideas of ADHD, he claimed that the children demonstrated little inhibitory volition. In other words, they showed a major defect in control that would make them prone to getting in trouble with the law later in life. He considered this a chronic condition and hypothesized that the problem was either hereditary or the result of some birth-related brain injury.

In the years 1917–1918, after an outbreak of encephalitis (a viral infection of the brain), some of the children who survived the disease showed behavioral and cognitive impairment—mainly hyperactivity, failure to control impulses, and impaired attention—the same symptoms that define ADHD today. Because many people thought the symptoms were a consequence of brain damage caused by the infection, they called the condition "minimal brain damage." Later, as cases of children with these symptoms accumulated during many years of study, and no biological damage could be detected in their brains, the name was changed to "minimal brain dysfunction."

The name for these symptoms—always with an emphasis on the hyperactivity component—changed over the following decades as researchers looked, without success, for a biological cause. Then, in 1950, a more pragmatic approach emerged. Researchers decided to describe the symptoms and, instead of looking for the cause, search for a way to improve them.

During the 1950s and 1960s, stimulant medication, psychotherapy, and parental counseling were the tools used to alleviate these symptoms. Later, in the 1970s, when

Figure 2.1 In 1902, British physician George Still (pictured here) became the first scientist to describe the condition we know today as ADHD. In a report before the Royal College of Medicine, Still described a group of children with behavioral problems he had studied. His theory was that the children's hyperactivity and aggression was caused by an injury to the brain, a hypothesis that turned out to be incorrect.

psychotherapy was discredited as a treatment, stimulants, mainly Ritalin, became the preferred and, often, the only treatment.

It was also during the 1970s that hyperactivity was dropped as a requirement for the condition, and the emphasis was placed instead on impulsivity and lack of attention. To reflect this, the name of the condition was changed from "hyperactive reaction of childhood" to "attention deficit disorder" (ADD). In 1987, hyperactivity was again included as a symptom, and ADD was renamed "attention-deficit/hyperactivity disorder (ADHD)." Being hyperactive was one of many traits defining ADHD, however—not an obligatory requirement for an ADHD diagnosis. What is interesting about the inclusion of the symptoms of lack of attention and impulsivity in the ADHD diagnosis is that all of these symptoms respond to stimulants. As Diller notes, it is as if "The diagnosis has evolved and expanded . . . to account for all the problems, behaviors and performance deficits that respond to stimulants."[7] In the book *Ritalin Nation*, Richard DeGrandpre agrees: "It appears likely that 'ADD' and earlier categories of behavioral deviances were built around the discovery of behavior-controlling drugs."[8]

DIAGNOSIS OF ADHD

Even today, after decades of research, it is not easy to decide whether a person has ADHD. ADHD is not a clearly defined disease, like strep throat or chicken pox. There is no laboratory test to diagnose it.

For a while, after the discovery of the impressive effects stimulants have on most ADHD symptoms, researchers thought stimulants themselves could be used as a test for ADHD. In other words, if the person's behavior improved while taking stimulants, then he or she had ADHD. If the person's behavior did not improve, then he or she did not have ADHD.

This belief has been proven inaccurate. As noted in Chapter 1, studies have shown that stimulants have the same effect on hyperactive and non-hyperactive children: Stimulants make all children calmer and better able to concentrate in the short term.

Currently, the most common way to determine whether a person has ADHD is by comparing his or her symptoms against the list included in the fourth edition of the *Diagnostic and Statistical Manual of Mental Disorders*, presented in Table 2.1. The symptoms on this list are separated into three groups corresponding to the three principal characteristics of ADHD: inattention, hyperactivity, and impulsivity. For a positive diagnosis, the person must show at least six of nine symptoms of inattention or at least six of nine behaviors indicating hyperactivity-impulsivity.

Although some doctors take the list literally as a diagnostic tool for ADHD, checking the patient's behavior against the list and counting the number of items for which he or she has tested positive, other physicians are more conservative. They believe diagnosis cannot be reduced to a mathematical, yes-or-no formula.

In addition, to give a yes or no answer to the questions in the list is not as straightforward as it would seem. How often is "often" anyway? In fact, what may be "often" for one person may be "rarely" for another, depending on his or her personality. The expression of the behaviors, too, may depend on the number of children in a classroom, the teacher's style of teaching, and many other factors that have nothing to do with the specific child. For example, it has been reported that teachers of smaller special education classes are less likely to consider a child's behavior disturbing than are teachers of larger, mainstream classes. Other people wonder about the borderline cases. For example, does a child have ADHD if he or she is positive for five items in both categories?

Some also worry about describing these symptoms as part of a disease state. All of the symptoms of ADHD exist in humans in a continuum; they are present, in some degree, in all of us. Also, symptoms such as fidgeting, not listening, losing things, getting distracted, and being noisy are seen in many children. Some researchers suggest that we are treating childhood itself as a disease. As Diller, the author of

(Continued on page 30)

Table 2.1 Diagnostic Criteria for ADHD as Specified in the DSM-IV

A. Either (1) or (2):

1. Six (or more) of the following symptoms of inattention have persisted for at least 6 months to a degree that is maladaptive and inconsistent with developmental level:

INATTENTION

a) often fails to give close attention to details or makes careless mistakes in schoolwork, work, or other activities

b) often has difficulty sustaining attention in tasks or play activities

c) often does not seem to listen when spoken to directly

d) often does not follow through on instructions and fails to finish schoolwork, chores, or duties in the workplace (not due to oppositional behavior or failure to understand instructions)

e) often has difficulty organizing tasks and activities

f) often avoids, dislikes, or is reluctant to engage in, tasks that require sustained mental effort (such as schoolwork or homework)

g) often loses things necessary for tasks or activities (e.g., toys, school assignments, pencils, books, or tools)

h) is often easily distracted by extraneous stimuli

i) is often forgetful in daily activities

2. Six (or more) of the following symptoms of hyperactivity-impulsivity have persisted for at least 6 months to a degree that is maladaptive and inconsistent with developmental level:

HYPERACTIVITY
a) often fidgets with hands or feet or squirms in seat
b) often leaves seat in classroom or in other situations in which remaining seated is expected
c) often runs about or climbs excessively in situations in which it is inappropriate (in adolescents or adults, may be limited to subjective feelings of restlessness)
d) often has difficulty playing or engaging in leisure activities quietly
e) is often "on the go" or often acts as if "driven by a motor"
f) often talks excessively

IMPULSIVITY
g) often blurts out answers before questions have been completed
h) often has difficulty awaiting turn
i) often interrupts or intrudes on others (e.g., butts into conversations or games)

B. Some hyperactivity-impulsive or inattentive symptoms that caused impairment were present before age 7 years.

C. Some impairment from the symptoms is present in two or more settings (e.g., at school [or work] and at home).

D. There must be clear evidence of clinically significant impairment in social, academic or occupational functioning.

E. The symptoms do not occur exclusively during the course of a pervasive development disorder, schizophrenia, or another psychotic disorder and are not better accounted for by another mental disorder (such as a mood, anxiety, dissociative, or personality disorder).

Source: American Psychiatric Association. *Diagnostic and Statistical Manual of Mental Disorders*, 4th ed. Washington, D.C.: American Psychiatric Association, 1994.

(Continued from page 27)

Running on Ritalin, testified in front of the U.S. Department of Justice in Washington, D.C.: "There is no question in my mind that Tom Sawyer and Huck Finn, in many Contra Costa (California) schools, would be carrying the diagnoses of ADHD and oppositional defiant disorder, and put on at least one medication, if not two."[9]

For all the reasons stated above, many people believe that an accurate diagnosis of ADHD cannot be achieved in a short visit to a doctor's office, but instead requires skillful detective work. It depends on the combined efforts of parents, teachers, psychologists, doctors, and possibly other professionals to gather information on as many aspects of the child's life and history as possible.

In fact, in a 1996 survey of more than 500 behavioral-developmental pediatricians, psychologists, and general pediatricians, only 9% reported using DSM criteria as the

RITALIN AND INSULIN

No one would argue that some children are more energetic and active than others and that this makes them more difficult to teach and control. Only in the last few decades, however, have these traits and their consequent behaviors of hyperactivity, inattention, and/or impulsivity been diagnosed as a medical condition and treated with Ritalin.

Although many pediatricians believe that depriving a hyperactive child of Ritalin is similar to, say, depriving a diabetic of insulin, others find this metaphor faulty. Diabetes, they argue, is a physiological disease, whereas ADHD is a collection of behaviors without a known biological cause. Although diabetes is caused in part by the lack of insulin, the brains of children with ADHD cannot suffer from a "lack of Ritalin." Unlike insulin, a hormone that naturally is produced in the body, Ritalin is an artificial drug.

only set of rules for making an ADHD diagnosis. Most were more influenced by other behaviors, such as acting out or learning problems.

GATHERING INFORMATION TO DIAGNOSE ADHD

In their book *Beyond Ritalin*, Garber and colleagues suggest several steps in the gathering of information toward an ADHD diagnosis. A modified version of their approach is as follows:

- **Step 1: Rule out medical problems as the cause of the observed symptoms.** A physical examination of the child must be performed first to rule out many conditions whose symptoms could mimic ADHD. Among these conditions are vision and hearing problems, lead poisoning, thyroid problems, allergies, neurological problems, parasites, diabetes, and hypoglycemia. Taking some medications, such as those for asthma, could make a child fidgety or distracted.

- **Step 2: Rule out other emotional problems.** Anxiety, depression, and thought disorders may interfere with attention and concentration or make the child so agitated that he or she may seem hyperactive. On the other hand, ADHD makes life so hard for some children that they may experience these disorders as a consequence of having ADHD. Only a skilled clinician can determine if the ADHD or the emotional problem came first, a necessary step in obtaining correct and effective treatment.

- **Step 3: Determine if the child has learning disabilities.** Sometimes, teachers refer children to a doctor believing they have ADHD because they are having trouble staying on task and completing work at school. In some cases, the reason for this behavior is that the child has a learning disability. A learning disability is defined first as a problem in learning that is not the result of low intelligence or poor teaching. It also relates to the way a person perceives, processes, or expresses information. For example, a child may have difficulty remembering directions that are given orally, but no problem at all performing more difficult tasks that do not include oral communication. Alternatively, the child may easily work with numbers, solving difficult math problems, but have difficulties with easy reading or writing tasks. Obviously, this kind of disability can interfere with learning. To complicate matters further, about one-third of children with ADHD also have learning disabilities. It is very important to determine if a child has a learning disability rather than jumping to the diagnosis of ADHD, because medication will not help a child with a learning disability.

- **Step 4: Compare the diagnostic criteria of the DSM to the characteristics of the child.** The DSM criteria for ADHD are listed in Table 2.1 on pages 28–29.

- **Step 5: Observe the child in as many settings as possible.** It is important to gather information about the child's behavior before completing the DSM questionnaire. The DSM requires that at least two settings must be considered. Many professionals have pointed to the artificiality of the doctor's office setting, where the child's behavior may not reflect his or her normal manner of behaving.

- **Step 6: Have a professional observe the child in the classroom.** It may be worth the effort to have a trained observer collect the data in the school setting. Teachers are human, and their reports, even in the best of cases, are subjective.

- **Step 7: Have a professional conduct a psycho-educational evaluation.** The professional must record learning potential and achievement levels in several areas, including math, language arts, spelling, written expression, and reading, and must record learning disabilities and gaps. Based on the information that is gathered, a professional is better able to determine whether the child has ADHD. It is important to understand that a diagnosis of ADHD is not an end in itself, but a starting point. The goal is to gain a better understanding of the child's behavior that will help the doctor give a personalized treatment, one with a higher rate of success.

Several rating scales have been published to gather information on children's behavior for both parents and teachers. The most frequently used scales are the Conners' Rating Scales. The original scale, published for parents in 1970, includes 93 questions that cover hyperactivity, immaturity, and emotional and behavioral factors. There are also several versions of the Conners' Rating Scales for teachers. The original one includes 39 items covering hyperactivity, conduct problems, and emotional-overindulgent, anxious-passive, asocial, and daydreaming-inattentive behaviors. An abbreviated form of the Conners' Rating Scale can be used at periodic intervals by both parents and teachers to measure the effects of medication.

Other rating scales for parents and teachers include the Child Behavior Checklist, which has two parts. The first part of the parents' version measures social activities; that of the teachers' version measures how the child is adapting in the classroom. The second part, in both versions, measures internal emotional problems, external conduct problems, and attention problems.

Rating scales designed exclusively for a school setting are the ADD-H Comprehensive Teacher Rating Scale; Continuous-Performance Tasks for Children, Adolescents, and Adults; the Gordon Diagnostic System; and the Test of Variables of Attention.

TREATMENT OF ADHD

The most common treatment for ADHD in the United States is the stimulant drug Ritalin in its different formulations. The drug is taken by 70% of all school-age children who are diagnosed with ADHD. Alternative medications to Ritalin are Dexedrine or Cylert.

Medication is not the only way to treat ADHD. In fact, at least 20 to 30% of children and adults with ADHD do not respond to stimulants. Why this happens is not clear, but it appears that people with symptoms of hyperactivity respond better to stimulants than people whose symptoms include lack of concentration, distractibility, and/or impulsivity.

Overall, studies show that Ritalin has an impressive short-term effect on improving behavior. Ritalin improves attention span, gross motor coordination, impulsivity, aggressiveness, handwriting, and compliance. It also improves learning in the short term, but no long-term improvement in academic success has been shown.

To study the long-term effects of medication, a long-term prospective study must be conducted. Prospective studies, which follow subjects over a period of many years, are difficult to perform. The results of the ones published to date have been disappointing. According to Diller:

> Studies beginning in the 1960s showed that children who took stimulants for hyperactivity (the name for ADD at the time) over several years did just as poorly in

later life as a group of hyperactive children who took no medication. Compared to children without hyperactivity, both groups were less likely to have finished high school or to be employed, and more likely to have problems with the law or to have drug or alcohol problems. A large percentage of the hyperactive group, medicated or not, did relatively well, but overall those in this category wound up struggling much more frequently than their normal peers.[10]

From this excerpt, it appears that taking Ritalin is not the key to a long-term improvement in the behavior of children with ADHD. A treatment using many modes, including educational intervention and counseling (behavioral and/or family therapy) for at least three years, seems to make more of a difference in behavior. When children on these treatments reached young adulthood, they were found to have fewer problems than those who only took medication.

Gaber and his colleagues, in the book *Beyond Ritalin*, suggest some simple educational and psychological changes that may improve the behavior and performance of a child with ADHD. A summary of their techniques follows:

1. **Modify the environment.** For example, at school, modifying the environment may include changing where the child sits in the classroom. Some children may need to sit in the front, where the teacher can give them closer attention, while others will do better sitting in the back of the room. Sitting in a circle can offer the ADHD child too many excuses for socialization. Similarly, sitting by an open window or by the pencil sharpener does not seem to be the ideal place for a child with ADHD. On the other hand, although sitting alone will provide fewer distractions for some children, a child prone to daydreaming should not sit alone.

2. **Change the routine.** Some children work better in the morning, and others in the afternoon. Scheduling the courses that require higher concentration accordingly can improve performance.

3. **Pair an ADHD child who has poor organizational skills with a buddy.** For older children, allow them to borrow notes from other students if they have problems writing.

4. **Consider carefully whether the teacher fits that particular student.** Some children respond better to certain teaching styles than others. A class with a low student-to-teacher ratio is also advantageous.

5. **At home, find the right place and time to do homework.** The child may need to unwind when coming home from school. He or she may prefer to do homework after dinner or in the morning.

6. **Change the task to increase productivity.** If the child has problems following directions, it may be better to give him or her one task at a time or to break the assignment into smaller tasks. It also may work best to alternate easier tasks with more difficult ones, to make eye contact with the child when giving the assignments, and, if fine motor skills are a problem, to minimize written assignments or let the child use a computer.

7. **Enhance positive responses.** If the child has problems reacting to the consequences of his or her actions, or tends to act impulsively, behavioral interventions that enhance positive responses immediately may work best. For example, give the child

specific, brief, positive comments when he or she is doing the right thing; praise good behavior; ignore negative attention-getting behavior; and give short but consistent time-outs for bad behavior.

In general, experience and research agree that, in the long run, an approach that combines the behavioral interventions described above with medication is more effective in treating ADHD symptoms than medication alone.

Diller offers an interesting approach to reach an appropriate treatment. He suggests asking children, if they could take a pill that would fix all their problems, what would this pill do? A child's answer to this question will provide the doctor with a clear idea of what the child wants to improve, and the treatment can be designed to reach these goals.

Another factor that seems to make a great difference in the success of ADHD individuals in adulthood is the choice of job or career. Although this is important for everyone, individuals with ADHD must carefully choose a job or career that fits their special needs. In general, jobs that require a high degree of concentration (such as an air traffic controller) or great attention to detail (for example, accounting or editing) are probably not appropriate for an individual with ADHD. People with ADHD tend do well in fast-changing, high-stress environments, such as the stock market or computer technology.

3

Ritalin and the Human Brain

ATTENTION-DEFICIT/HYPERACTIVITY DISORDER: SYMPTOMS IN SEARCH OF A CAUSE

The symptoms of inattention, distractibility, and/or hyperactivity that define attention-deficit/hyperactivity disorder (ADHD) improve when treated with the stimulant drug Ritalin. For long-term success, however, the behaviors associated with these symptoms can also addressed with different techniques, some of which have been described in Chapter 2.

These two different types of treatments point to two different causes for ADHD. The improvement observed when taking a chemical substance seems to indicate that ADHD has a biological cause. However, improvement by behavioral modification techniques suggests that ADHD may have an environmental cause.

ADHD: A BIOLOGICAL CAUSE?

The prevalent theory among both health professionals and the general public today is that the symptoms of ADHD have a biological cause. The most generally cited causes are birth defects, an infant trauma, and the brain's inability to produce enough of specific neurotransmitters, or brain chemical messengers.

The widespread use of expressions such as "He has a chemical imbalance" or "Her brain is hard-wired this way" when talking about children considered to have ADHD reinforces this belief. Although the lingo may be new, the theory of a biological cause for ADHD-like behavior is more than 100 years old. In 1902, the British physician George Still attributed the aggressive and defiant behavior of the children he was studying to either a genetic cause or some birth-related injury. Brain damage was also thought to be the cause of the behavioral problems experienced by the children who had survived the encephalitis outbreak of 1917–1918. As late as the 1950s, symptoms similar to the ones now included in ADHD were grouped under the term *minimal brain damage*. This physiological brain damage was never found, and eventually the term was abandoned. The search for a biological cause for ADHD, however, was not.

Although there is evidence that ADHD is hereditary, it has proven difficult to separate the effects of genetic inheritance from those of family environment. The only data pointing to a genetic component for ADHD have been compiled when working with identical twins. These studies found that it was more likely for identical twins to meet ADHD criteria than it was for fraternal twins. Since, by definition, identical twins have the same genetic material, this indicated that at least part of the ADHD condition is genetic. Yet the probability for one identical twin to have ADHD if the other had it was less than one in three. Moreover, to date, no specific gene for ADHD behavior has been identified.

Using different techniques of brain imaging, several groups of researchers have looked for differences between the brains of ADHD and non-ADHD individuals. In one of the best-known studies, Alan Zametkin and his colleagues at the National Institute of Mental Health used positron emission tomography (PET) scanning to evaluate glucose metabolism in the brain. Because glucose is the only source of energy for the brain, the way the brain uses glucose can serve as a gross indicator of activity in its various parts.

For the studies, patients were given radioactive glucose. Because of the high level of radiation associated with this technique, the studies were not done on children but on adults thought to have suffered from ADHD as children. The results, published in the *New England Journal of Medicine* in 1990, showed a 8.1% decrease in brain metabolism, meaning that glucose was underutilized, in the group who had ADHD as children compared with those who did not.[11] This difference in the rate of metabolism led scientists to the conclusion that they had located a biological cause for ADHD.

Magazines and newspapers embraced this conclusion eagerly. After all, how can you argue with a brain scan? *Time* magazine, in an article called "Why Junior Won't Sit Still," noted that in a "landmark study that could help put to rest decades of confusion and controversy, researchers at the NIMW have traced ADD . . . to a specific metabolic abnormality in the brain."[12] The *New York Times*, *Washington Post*, and *Newsweek* joined in the reporting of this apparent breakthrough.

Despite the buzz, not everyone was convinced that the results proved that ADHD has a biological basis. First, efforts to replicate these findings have failed. Second, the participants were adults, not children, which limits the applicability. Third, there is no evidence that an 8.1% difference in brain metabolism produces a significant difference in behavior, including hyperactivity. In fact, this difference in metabolism did not correlate with performance on an attention task. Fourth, 72% of participants in the hyperactive group were men, compared with the control group, which was only 56%. When another group of researchers compared the metabolism of men and women in the control group of the Zametkin study, they found the statistical difference to be the same as the one they had found between the control and the hyperactive groups. This means that the difference between the hyperactive and control group in Zametkin's study could be the result of the hyperactive group having a larger percentage of males. Finally, even if the difference in brain metabolism between the two groups were real, this does not mean the decreased metabolism is the cause of the hyperactivity.

In 1993, Zametkin and colleagues published a follow-up study in which they performed PET scanning to measure glucose metabolism in the brains of ADHD and non-ADHD adolescents. This time, they found no difference between the brains of the ADHD adolescents and the non-ADHD adolescents.

In a later study, they looked at the glucose metabolism in the brain of ADHD individuals before and after taking Ritalin. The idea was that if ADHD symptoms are caused by a decrease on glucose metabolism and Ritalin improves ADHD symptoms (their hypothesis), then taking Ritalin would increase glucose metabolism. Again, their results failed to show any change.

Even Zametkin has admitted that PET scanning cannot tell whether a person is ADHD. "One commonly asked question of our brain imaging studies," he has stated, "is whether PET scanning can be used to diagnose ADHD. Unfortunately, this is not currently possible because there is considerable overlap in our study between normal and ADHD brain metabolism." [13]

Yet, because Zametkin's follow-up studies did not reach the press, his first results were never challenged publicly, and PET scans are still mentioned today as the ultimate proof for the biological cause of ADHD. As an example, psychoanalyst Frederick Fisher, as recently as March 16, 2003, stated in the *Philadelphia Inquirer* magazine that ADHD "is a demonstrable organic condition that shows up on PET (positron emission tomography) scans involving glucose metabolism." [14]

Two Californian physicians, Daniel Amen and Blake Carmichael, have used another radiological technique—single photon emission computed tomography (SPECT) scanning—on more than 2,000 patients, including adolescents and children. This process, which uses less radiation than PET, detects variation in blood flow (and indirectly detects biochemical activity) in the brain. These researchers claim there is a correlation between ADHD and decreased blood flow in the tissues of the prefrontal cortex (Figure 3.1). Although other experts have criticized the lack of reproducibility of this study, Amen believes the scanning is evidence of the biological nature of ADHD and uses it to diagnose ADHD.

In summary, no reliable scientific evidence for the biological cause of ADHD has been found to date. Zametkin, the researcher behind the PET scan studies on the brain, agrees:

> Could it be that a dysfunction of the central nervous system is the key to our understanding of the etiology of attention deficit disorder? Individually, each finding is insufficient to prove that ADHD has a neurobiological basis. Indeed, it may still be a long time until the underlying cause of ADHD is established.[15]

ADHD AND THE ENVIRONMENT: NATURE VERSUS NURTURE

In the book *The Music of Dolphins*, Karen Hesse tells the story of a girl raised by dolphins from the age of four. Rescued as a teenager, she is taught how to talk and behave like a human. Although she progresses to a point where she is able to communicate, she cannot become fully integrated into a society she still perceives as alien.

This story, which closely follows the modern theories about speech and behavior development, shows how much influence the environment has in shaping the self. In other words, the story shows the importance of the nurture part in the old argument of nurture (the influence of environment) versus nature (the influence of genetic makeup). Although the girl in the book had the genetic makeup to be human, without

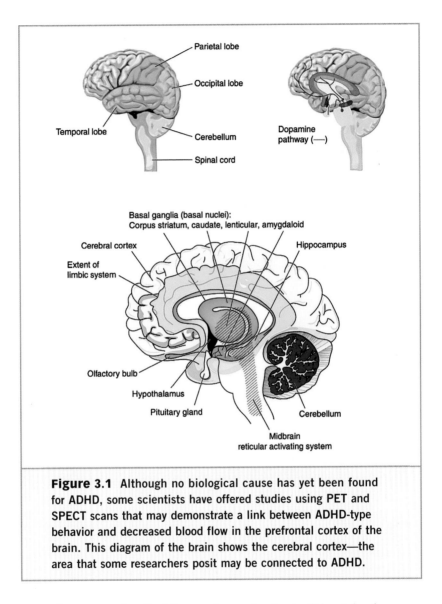

Parietal lobe

Occipital lobe

Temporal lobe

Cerebellum

Spinal cord

Dopamine
pathway (——)

Basal ganglia (basal nuclei):
Corpus striatum, caudate, lenticular, amygdaloid

Cerebral cortex

Hippocampus

Extent of
limbic system

Olfactory bulb

Hypothalamus

Pituitary gland

Cerebellum

Midbrain
reticular activating system

Figure 3.1 Although no biological cause has yet been found for ADHD, some scientists have offered studies using PET and SPECT scans that may demonstrate a link between ADHD-type behavior and decreased blood flow in the prefrontal cortex of the brain. This diagram of the brain shows the cerebral cortex—the area that some researchers posit may be connected to ADHD.

the proper stimuli while growing up, her brain did not develop to its full potential.

As Daniel Goleman writes in his book *Emotional Intelligence*, there is increasing evidence that to develop in a healthy way, a child's brain needs real-life experiences. The experiences after birth, rather than something innate, determine the actual "wiring" of the human brain. "Wiring" refers here to the connection the neurons (brain cells) make with one another (Figure 3.2). If we consider that the human brain is composed of about 10 to 100 billion neurons, and that these neurons make thousands of connections with other neurons, we come up with a web of billions of connections. These connections, however, are not present in the newborn baby's brain. In the newborn's brain, about 4.7 million branches grow out from neuron to neuron every minute. Although the genome has a role in this complex process, it is the moment-to-moment experience of the child that determines which connections will remain and which will be cut.

Many examples suggest this plasticity. For example, if a child with a lazy eye covers the healthy eye, eventually the vision in the weaker eye improves because the neurons grow new connections to reinforce the path to the weaker eye. A child born in China learns to speak Chinese, while the same child raised in England would learn to speak English. Although every child growing up in Spain knows how to roll the "r," it is difficult for an adult nonnative speaker to learn to do so.

If environmental influences can actually alter brain functions and shape behavior, it is not surprising that many people believe a child's early experiences have an effect on whether he or she develops ADHD. In other words, some experts contend that the environment can cause or change ADHD.

Several studies support this theory. One of them, published in 1995, observed 191 children at 6-month intervals during early and middle childhood. The study found that variables operating at the level of the family (mainly, quality of care giving, parents' marital status at the time of the child's birth, emotional support given to the caregivers, and the caregiving style) were good indicators of which children would or would not show ADHD-related problems. The results indicated that the child's early experiences do have an effect on the development of ADHD.[16]

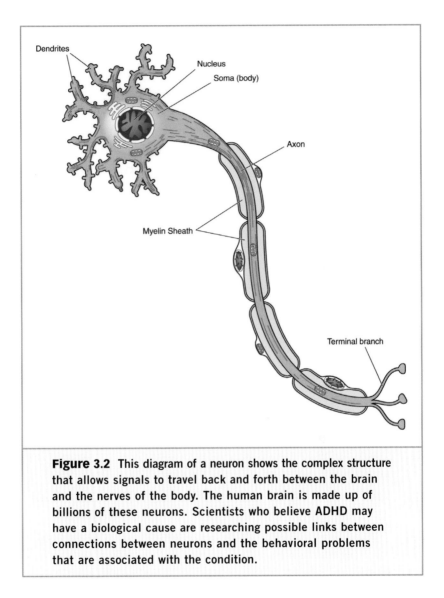

Figure 3.2 This diagram of a neuron shows the complex structure that allows signals to travel back and forth between the brain and the nerves of the body. The human brain is made up of billions of these neurons. Scientists who believe ADHD may have a biological cause are researching possible links between connections between neurons and the behavioral problems that are associated with the condition.

THE "BIOPSYCHOSOCIAL" MODEL

If the biological cause for the ADHD behavior is accepted, the use of medication as a "cure" easily follows. If, on the other hand, emotional or relational problems are considered the cause, medication is no longer the simple cure, and the techniques offered for improvement (psychological and social approaches) are longer and more time-consuming.

The biological cause model remains popular because a solution in pill form is appealing and because accepting a biological cause removes blame from parents. Yet to believe only in a genetic and neurological cause for the disorder would entail ignoring many environmental factors, such as learning disabilities, emotional problems, family dynamics, classroom size, and economic and cultural issues, which may also be of significance in the development of ADHD.

Lawrence Diller believes that neither the genetic model nor the environment model alone provides the whole picture for ADHD. Instead, he argues that a "biopsychosocial model," in which several factors—including a person's biology, emotional status, and environment interact—provides a better solution. In this model, the path between the mind and the body is seen as a two-way street: The brain affects emotions and behavior and, in turn, the brain is affected by the person's experiences. After all, although everyone is born with a basic personality, it is the experiences an individual has while growing up that will shape him or her into the kind of person he or she will become.

EFFECT OF RITALIN ON THE BRAIN

Regardless of what causes ADHD, the behavior of a person with ADHD improves in the short term after taking a stimulant drug such as Ritalin. Ritalin also improves concentration, increases attention span, and lowers the activity level both in individuals with ADHD and without. On the other hand, Ritalin may cause several adverse drug reactions, from growth inhibition to psychosis.

How Ritalin accomplishes these changes is not completely understood. Nonetheless, several studies have shown that stimulants affect the structure, biochemistry, blood flow, and energy utilization of the brain. The areas of the brain affected

Table 3.1 Effect of Stimulants in Various Areas of the Brain

AREA OF BRAIN	EFFECTS OF STIMULANTS
Basal Ganglia	Abnormal movements (i.e., trouble walking), impaired emotional capacity
Cerebellum	Impaired coordination
Cerebral Cortex	Impairment of higher mental activities, such as intelligence and sensory perception
Frontal Lobe	Reasoning, judgment, and emotional impairment
Hippocampus	Impairment of memory and learning
Hypothalamus	Impairment of temperature and hormone regulation, appetite problems
Limbic System	Emotional dysfunction
Parietal Lobe	Impairment of sensory perception
Pituitary Gland	Growth problems, sexual dysfunction
Reticular Activating System	Impaired responsiveness, alertness, and self-awareness
Spinal Cord	Impaired muscle tone and movement
Temporal Lobe	Impairment of memory and learning

by stimulants are shown in Figure 3.1 on page 43. Table 3.1 summarizes the effect of stimulants in various areas of the brain.

On a physiological level, Ritalin causes a 23 to 30% decrease of the overall blood flow in all areas of the human brain, as measured by a PET scan. This reduction is believed to be caused by a constriction of the blood vessels, probably related to Ritalin's impact on the neurotransmitter dopamine. Ritalin also has a significant effect on glucose metabolism in the brain. As noted previously, since glucose is the only source of energy in the brain, its metabolism is directly related to the brain's overall energy consumption. At the lowest dosage, Ritalin increases energy consumption in many areas of the brain that are central to motor activity and mental function. Most of these areas are dopamine pathways.

Other studies suggest that in the long term, Ritalin may also cause cortical atrophy, which refers to the withering and shrinking of brain tissue. This finding poses great concern, since the cortex of the brain is critical to higher mental function, including intelligence.

EFFECT OF RITALIN ON NEUROTRANSMITTERS

The brain is composed of cells called neurons. Unlike other cells in the body, neurons do not touch each other. The connection between any two neurons is made through neurotransmitters, chemicals that act as messengers.

Neurotransmitters are very small molecules. They are released from the tip of the neuron extension, or axon, into the space (called a synapse) that separates individual neurons (Figure 3.3). As a result, electrical impulses travel down the neuron membranes. Once neurotransmitters are released, they travel through the synapse until they are picked up by receptors in the neighboring cells. Some neurotransmitters decrease (inhibit) activity, while others increase (excite) activity of the neuron to which they bind. Any particular neuron may be surrounded by thousands of others that are, at any given moment, releasing neurotransmitters. The neuron must weigh the relative strengths of the inhibitory and excitatory signals of these neurotransmitters to determine when a signal should be sent down its axon.

Ritalin interferes with this complex neurotransmitter system both by increasing the number of neurotransmitters released

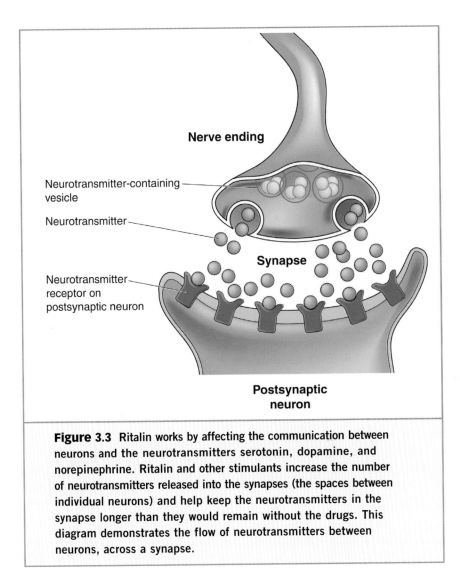

Figure 3.3 Ritalin works by affecting the communication between neurons and the neurotransmitters serotonin, dopamine, and norepinephrine. Ritalin and other stimulants increase the number of neurotransmitters released into the synapses (the spaces between individual neurons) and help keep the neurotransmitters in the synapse longer than they would remain without the drugs. This diagram demonstrates the flow of neurotransmitters between neurons, across a synapse.

in the synapses and by reducing the rate of their removal, so that the neurotransmitters stay in the synaptic space longer.

Different neurons synthesize and release different neuro-transmitters into the synapses. Ritalin and other stimulants interact with the neurons that produce and respond to the neurotransmitters dopamine, norepinephrine, and serotonin.

DOPAMINE

The activation of the dopamine pathways in the brain, researchers believe, produces the therapeutic effect of suppressing spontaneity as well as the most serious adverse effects of drug abuse and addiction. These effects occur because the neurons that release dopamine originate in two areas deep within the brain: the substantia nigra and the ventral tegmentum. Dopamine neurons in the substantia nigra reach into the basal ganglia, which control motor activity and influence mental processes. These ganglia are connected to the reticular activating system that is the energizing core of the brain and the limbic system that regulates emotions. Dopamine neurons from the ventral tegmentum go directly to the centers of the brain that control thinking and feeling, including the frontal lobes and limbic system. The dopamine system thus affects portions of the brain involved with the processes most essential to being human.

Dopamine neurons also go to the hypothalamus and pituitary glands. There, they control the hormonal processes involved in growth and reproductive functioning.

NOREPINEPHRINE

Ritalin also stimulates neurons that release norepinephrine into the synapse. This is believed to result in overactivity of the cardiovascular system and some symptoms of drug withdrawal. Most of the norepinephrine-generating neurons originate in the locus coeruleus of the brain. This locus is connected to the cerebral cortex and the reticular activating system.

SEROTONIN

By increasing the activity of the neurotransmitter serotonin, Ritalin affects both higher human activities and basic physiological functions. In fact, increasing serotonin levels affects every brain function described in Table 3.1 on page 47. Some researchers believe that Ritalin produces more extreme mental aberrations, including psychosis and delusions, by affecting the serotonin pathways in the brain.

The relationship between Ritalin and the overall mental function of the brain is far from being well understood. Dopamine, norepinephrine, and serotonin—the neurotransmitters known to be affected by Ritalin—are only three of the hundreds of substances that control brain functioning.

The brain does not welcome external molecules. It sees them as intruders and tries to compensate for their effect. In the case of stimulant drugs, the brain reacts to the excess of neurotransmitters in the synapse in two ways:

1. The neuron releasing the neurotransmitter receives feedback signals that cause it to shut down, causing less neurotransmitter to be released into the synaptic space.

2. The neuron receiving the neurotransmitter tries to reduce the amount of stimuli by destroying the receptors that bind to that particular neurotransmitter. The disappearance of the receptors has actually been measured in experiments with animals.

Sometimes, these compensatory changes in the brain become permanent, causing irreversible malfunction.

In summary, although its advocates claim that Ritalin corrects an imbalance in the brain or enhances brain function, the reality is not so simple. The only thing certain is that Ritalin, like any external substance that reaches the brain, has a high probability of disrupting the normal mental process in unexpected ways.

4

Trends in Ritalin Use

RITALIN USE IN CHILDREN

The trend in Ritalin use has changed dramatically during the last decade. The number of people diagnosed as having attention-deficit/hyperactivity disorder (ADHD) has increased from 900,000 in 1990 to about 5 million in 2000. At the same time, the number of prescriptions for Ritalin has increased from 3 million in 1991 to 11 million in 1998. In addition, the age and the type of individuals diagnosed as having ADHD has also changed.

As late as the 1980s, ADHD was considered a childhood problem. The majority of children diagnosed with the disorder had very severe symptoms, of which hyperactivity was obligatory. According to Diller in his book *Running on Ritalin*, the typical profile of an ADHD sufferer in the 1980s consisted of "boys from six to 12 years old, extremely hyperactive and impulsive, functioning poorly (if at all) in a normal school situation. Many were quite out of control, and Ritalin was often needed to give other treatments a chance to work."[17]

Parents were confused about their inability to improve their child's behavior and blamed themselves for this failure. In most cases, they had not heard of ADHD. Some parents, especially fathers, refused to believe there could be something wrong with their child's brain and blamed the mother's parenting style for

the problem. Often, parents refused to give their child a stimulant drug and had to be coerced into doing so.

The situation is quite different now. Today, everybody seems to know about ADHD, and Ritalin is widely accepted as a "miracle pill" that makes children behave. This belief is so widespread that some parents cannot wait for their children to turn six, the recommended age for a child to start receiving Ritalin. In fact, some do not wait, and, although it is against the American Psychiatric Association's recommendations, the number of children under the age of six taking Ritalin is increasing.

Nowadays, when parents call the doctor to make an appointment, they may already have decided that their child

A QUESTION OF CANNOT VERSUS WILL NOT?

When, after years of struggling with their child's behavior, parents ask a doctor whether their child has ADHD, what they are really asking is whether there is a physiological reason for their child to behave the way he or she does. What they are asking is whether the child *cannot* behave or whether he or she *will not* behave.

Tired of blaming themselves for what they see as their own failure, parents are often eager to embrace the idea that there is some malfunction in the child's brain that puts the desired behavior outside of his or her control. If the cause of the behavior is biological, the child is physically unable to behave differently and the parents are not at fault. If the cause is psychological, on the other hand, this implies an emotional or relational problem, one for which parents might be considered partly responsible.

In the first case, taking a pill is readily justified. In the second, there is no easy cure. This accounts for the allure of a biological cause for ADHD.

has ADHD and should be taking Ritalin. Many ask directly whether the doctor will perform ADHD tests. If the doctor tells them that an "ADHD test" does not exist, they will take their child to another doctor. If this particular doctor does not give their child a prescription for Ritalin, they will take the child elsewhere until they find a doctor who does.

It is not surprising, then, that the number of children diagnosed with ADHD and taking Ritalin has increased. Between 2 and 3.5% of children in the United States are taking Ritalin; in some schools, the figure is as high as 18%.

These numbers make some people uneasy. But others, such as Joseph Biederman, believe this increase is a positive development because it means child psychiatry is finally recognizing the need for medication. According to Biederman, 10% of American children have ADHD, which means the condition is actually underdiagnosed. If all these children were prescribed Ritalin, the current treatment rates would double.

Parents are not the only ones responsible for the increase in Ritalin use. In some cases, schools will not allow children diagnosed with ADHD into the classroom if they are not on Ritalin. In the case of divorced parents, one court reportedly took custody away from a father because he would not agree to give Ritalin to his child.

The profile of the children described as ADHD sufferers has changed, too. Although some of the children have problems at home or school, more often, children who are not hyperactive and who may function normally at school are diagnosed with ADHD. These children are identified for their inability to pay attention and get their work done, or because they have problems with daydreaming, concentration, or getting organized.

Today, parents embrace the ADHD diagnosis with relief because, following the prevailing theory, they accept that the

child's problems are caused by his or her inherent brain chemistry, which means that they, as parents, are not to blame. Instead of having to be coerced to give Ritalin to their children, many parents are eager to do so.

A very telling example of this change in the popular trend is exemplified by the fact that parents, teachers, and children refer to the condition as "having ADHD" or "being ADHD." By doing this, they reinforce the validity of the condition as a medical disorder and ignore the slippery nature of the diagnosis; they ignore the fact that ADHD is not a disease itself but a metaphorical construct that refers to a wide array of symptoms. Even the phrase "having ADHD" (as in "having" asthma or diabetes) implies the condition is a disease state, and therefore biologically based, discounting the possible effects of the environment. This overlooks the possibility that the child's behavior may be a result of how the child has been or is being treated. Because ADHD is often viewed as a disease state, the affected children are prescribed Ritalin, but nothing is done to change the environment that may also be influencing their behavior. The fact is that there may be nothing inherently wrong with the child. It is possible that all that is needed is a change in parenting style, teaching, or the child's social environment.

PROUD OF HAVING ADHD: A NEW TREND

Another important distinction between diseases such as diabetes and asthma as opposed to ADHD is that the two former conditions are malfunctions of the body. As such, they do not define the personality of the individual who suffers from them the way ADHD, a malfunction of the brain, does. Perhaps that is why most children under the age of 10 do not like to take Ritalin. These children do not like the way it makes them feel and are worried about being teased by their peers or perceived as crazy. The fact that they have to go to the nurse's office to receive a second dose

of Ritalin during the school day reinforces these feelings by making their condition public.

Not only can taking Ritalin be damaging to children's self-esteem, but being labeled with ADHD cause problems, too. A Ritalin prescription implies that ADHD has a biological origin, that there is a chemical imbalance in the child's brain, and that an external drug is needed to fix it. If this is true, then what children are being told is that there is something wrong with them at a very basic level. Because Ritalin does not cure ADHD, but only helps control the symptoms, the implication is that what is wrong with the children's brains will never change and that they will have to take medication forever. It is not surprising that children often have low self-esteem under these circumstances.

Low self-esteem may be the reason why many children refuse to continue taking medication by the time they reach the age of 12 or 13. The fact that children with more severe symptoms are the ones who are most eager to reject Ritalin seems to support this theory, because these children are probably the ones with lower self-esteem.

Interestingly enough, when it comes to teenagers and adults with ADHD, the situation is quite different. Many teenagers and adults view the fact that they have ADHD as a positive trait. Books like *Driven to Distraction* by Hallowell and Ratey may be partly responsible for this change in attitude toward taking Ritalin. By introducing into the public main-stream the concept that along with the negative traits, ADHD individuals possess many positive characteristics, Hallowell and Ratey are attempting to remove the stigma associated with ADHD. In fact, Hallowell, who claims to have ADHD, defines the disorder as having "an indefinable, zany sense of life." Talking about one of his patients, he says, "Like many ADDers, he was intuitive, warm, and empathic."

In Hallowell's own words, ADHD is a desirable state: "Instead of thinking of myself as having a character flaw,

a family legacy, or some potentially ominous 'difference' between me and other people, I could see myself in terms of having a unique brain biology. . . . In fact, I would much rather have ADD than not have it, since I love the positive qualities that go along with it—creativity, energy, and unpredictability." [18, 19]

Many groups have appeared over the last few years that define themselves as "proud of being ADHD." These run the gamut from authors like Hallowell, who believes ADHD gives him a different, positive perception of life, to Thom Harmann, author of *Attention Deficit Disorder: A Different Perception,* who claims that ADHD "is an inherited set of skills," [20] to many Web sites that celebrate ADHD creativity. These people believe themselves to be distinctively different from the non-ADHD population in terms of learning abilities, outlook on life, and creativity. They view their ADHD qualities, once thought to be only a negative burden, as assets.

This does beg the question that if being ADHD bestows positive traits, why would individuals with the disorder want to take medication for it?

RITALIN USE BEYOND CHILDHOOD

During the 1980s, children diagnosed with ADHD were expected to outgrow their symptoms, and generally stopped taking Ritalin by the time they reached puberty. Follow-up studies discovered, however, that although the symptoms of hyperactivity and impulsivity decreased to some extent with age, many children—between 30 and 80%, depending on the estimates—continued to struggle during adolescence and adulthood. The fact that children do not always outgrow their ADHD symptoms after reaching puberty is one of the factors that have contributed to the increase in the incidence of ADHD and, consequently, of Ritalin use among the adult population.

Other factors include the shift in the definition of ADHD in the latest edition of the *Diagnostic and Statistical Manual of Mental Disorders* from excessive motor activity and impulsivity to inattention. Without hyperactivity as a requirement, many adults began to recognize aspects of ADHD in themselves when their own child was diagnosed with the disorder and started to take medication. In addition, several popular books, such as Hallowell and Ratey's *Driven to Distraction*, include lists of possible traits for the ADHD personality. Although the authors insist that their list is not intended to be a self-test, people began to use the list to diagnose themselves. The traits are so general that nearly everyone can relate to them. For example, the first 10 items on the list from their book are: [21]

1. Are you left-handed or ambidextrous?

2. Do you have a family history of drug or alcohol abuse, depression, or manic-depressive illness?

3. Are you moody?

4. Were you considered an underachiever in school? Now?

5. Do you have trouble getting started on things?

6. Do you drum your fingers a lot, tap your feet, fidget, or pace?

7. When you read, do you find that you often have to reread an entire paragraph or an entire page because you were daydreaming?

8. Do you tune out or space out a lot?

9. Do you have a hard time relaxing?

10. Are you excessively impatient?

Upon reading the book and taking the test, many adults recognized a pattern in the problems with which they had struggled all their lives, problems that might have affected their work and home lives. Still, Ritalin use in adults is low compared to that in children. As of 1995, IMS America Ltd., a commercial drug-surveying company, reported that only 25% of all individuals taking Ritalin were adults.

DEMOGRAPHICS OF RITALIN USE

According to Diller, author of *Running on Ritalin,* "The families [who bring their children to his practice thinking ADHD is behind their problematic behavior] are mostly white, middle- and upper-middle class. In nearly all cases, at least one parent has a job; in most families, both parents are working." [22]

This description agrees with the general trend. Overall, the Ritalin boom appears to be primarily a North American, white, middle- to upper-middle-class, suburban phenomenon. The majority of the children diagnosed with ADHD are boys, and minorities are underrepresented.

Geography

The United States produces and uses about 85% of the world's total Ritalin supply. Although Ritalin consumption in Canada quadrupled between 1990 and 1996, it still remains less than one-half of that in the United States. Australia is the only other country to note a similarly large increase in the use of Ritalin during the 1990s, although that nation's rate of usage remains only one-tenth that of the United States.

None of the industrialized nations of Asia has experienced a recent increase in the use of stimulants. In Europe, the prevalence rates run as low as one-tenth of 1%. Even in England, where Ritalin's use has increased over 20-fold since 1990, children are from 10 to 50 times less likely to be diagnosed with ADHD than in the United States (Figure 4.1).

Within the United States, rates of Ritalin use vary from state to state and from community to community. This variability is known because the Drug Enforcement Administration

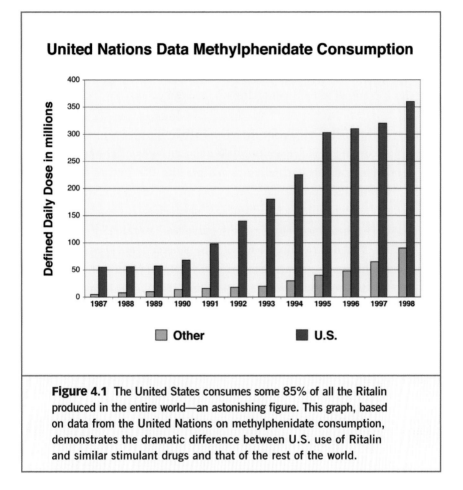

United Nations Data Methylphenidate Consumption

Figure 4.1 The United States consumes some 85% of all the Ritalin produced in the entire world—an astonishing figure. This graph, based on data from the United Nations on methylphenidate consumption, demonstrates the dramatic difference between U.S. use of Ritalin and similar stimulant drugs and that of the rest of the world.

(DEA) has a system called the Automation of Reports and Consolidated Orders System (ARCOS) that tracks Schedule II controlled substances from manufacturer to consumer. This system can be used to determine the amount of Ritalin used in different locations, on a per capita basis in entire states or by zip code areas within a state.

Although most experts believe the prevalence of ADHD in the United States to be between 3 and 5% of the population, ARCOS data, prescription data, and epidemiological studies have identified large differences between communities. Some areas report almost no use of Ritalin, whereas in other places, 10 to 20% of students receive stimulants for ADHD treatment. For instance, in 1996, in Virginia Beach, Virginia, Ritalin use among white fifth-grade boys was 17%, or one in six boys district-wide.

Table 4.1 ranks the states with the highest use of methylphenidate per 100,000 people. Although average Ritalin use is 3,082 grams per 100,000 people, California and Hawaii have the lowest per capita use, with 1,748 and 1,208 grams per 100,000 people, respectively.

Gender

The majority of the children diagnosed with ADHD are boys. Data from the U.S. Census in 1994 estimated that 5.8% of boys and 1.5% of girls age 5 to 17 had been labeled ADHD by their physicians.

Race and Ethnicity

Minorities are underrepresented among individuals with ADHD. For example, several surveys show that African-American

RITALIN MILLS

One of the contributors to the Ritalin boom of the last decade has been the so-called Ritalin mills—that is, those clinics or practices where the main role of the physician is to diagnose ADHD and prescribe Ritalin.

Although there is no direct proof of the existence of "Ritalin mills," the following numbers point to the possibility that a small number of doctors are responsible for writing most of the prescriptions for Ritalin. In Michigan, a survey of pre-scriptions found that 5% of the pediatricians had prescribed 50% of the Ritalin in the state. In Delaware, 6% of purchasers (which include clinics, physicians, and pharmacies) wrote 26.2% of Ritalin prescriptions. In Virginia, 2 out of 1,309 providers, or an astonishing 0.01%, wrote 26% of the Ritalin prescriptions for the entire state.

Table 4.1 1999 Methylphenidate Distibution: Top 10 Users
DEA ARCOS DATA

RANK	STATE	GRAMS PER 100K
1	New Hampshire	5,525
2	Vermont	5,005
3	Michigan	4,848
4	Iowa	4,638
5	Delaware	4,439
6	Massachusetts	4,318
7	South Dakota	4,235
8	Virginia	4,207
9	Minnesota	3,941
10	Maryland	3,935

Source: Congressional Testimony. Statement by Terrance Woodworth before the Committee on Education and the Workforce: Subcommittee on Early Childhood, Youth and Families, May 16, 2000. Available online at *http://www.usdoj.gov/dea/pubs/cngrtest/ct051600.htm.*

children are both diagnosed with ADHD and prescribed Ritalin less frequently than Caucasian children. This difference may be because of cultural and economic issues. African Americans may be less willing to bring their children to medical specialists for behavior and performance problems.[23] Another reason may be that because of crack cocaine usage and problems among the African-American community, parents are apprehensive about giving stimulants to their children. They may also be skeptical of an educational system they perceive as too ready to find fault in the behavior of their children, judged by the standards of what they see as a white-dominated society.

The incidence of ADHD in Asian children is also low. This difference may be because methods of disciplining children differ between Asian-American parents and Caucasian-American parents. It may also be because Asian Americans are less comfortable than their Caucasian counterparts are with the American mental health system and its willingness to prescribe drugs to treat mental conditions.

5

Ritalin Abuse

RITALIN, COCAINE, AND AMPHETAMINES
SHARE THE SAME PATTERN

Ritalin has been hailed by many parents and teachers as a miracle pill once described by its makers (Novartis, formerly Ciba-Geigy Pharmaceuticals) as "a mild central nervous system stimulant" and by the *New York Times* as a "mild stimulant" that is "roughly [equivalent to] a jolt of strong coffee."[24] These statements belie the fact that Ritalin has been known, since it was first marketed in the mid-1950s, to be a highly addictive drug subject to widespread abuse.

Ritalin abuse and addiction were reported during the 1960s and 1970s in the United States and Japan. Ritalin was marketed as a weight-loss product in Sweden in the 1960s, but its abuse as a street drug created an epidemic of such magnitude that the Swedish government was forced to ban its use in 1968. In the United States in the 1970s, the FDA and the National Academy of Sciences warned that Ritalin was developing a black-market value as a recreational stimulant. Yet the warning did not prevent the boom in Ritalin that was legally prescribed for children with ADHD over the following decades.

Since 1971, the DEA has described Ritalin as a powerful stimulant that "shares many of the pharmacological effects of amphetamine, methamphetamine, and cocaine." The American Psychiatric Association (APA) agrees. In its book *Treatments of Psychiatric Disorders* (1989), the association states that Ritalin is neuropharmacologically similar to cocaine and amphetamines, and that all three drugs share the same abuse patterns. The *Diagnostic and Statistic*

Manual of Mental Disorders, also published by the APA, places cocaine, amphetamine, and Ritalin abuse and addiction in the same category. Furthermore, in 1995, N. D. Volkow and his colleagues at the Brookhaven National Laboratory discovered through PET scans that the way cocaine and Ritalin are distributed in the brain is identical, but that Ritalin remains in the body longer. In 1997, they summarized their research by stating that Ritalin, like cocaine, inhibits dopamine uptake by neurons, thus increasing the amount of dopamine left in the synapses. Thus, Ritalin produces the same high and the same reinforcing effects as cocaine.[25]

EFFECTS OF RITALIN ABUSE: FROM "HIGH" TO SUICIDAL DEPRESSION AND DEATH

An increasing number of adolescents are using Ritalin outside of its prescribed use to improve their concentration and study longer (performance enhancement), to get high (recreational use), or to suppress their appetite in the hope of losing weight (cosmetic use). They call Ritalin by a number of names, including Vitamin R, Rit, R-ball, the smart drug, poor man's cocaine, or kiddie coke. Adolescents use the drug by swallowing it as a pill, crushing it and snorting it like cocaine, or dissolving it in water and injecting it like heroin.

According to the Clearinghouse Fact Series, the effects of intoxication with Ritalin are:[26]

- Loss of appetite (which may cause serious malnutrition),

- Tremors and muscle twitching,

- Fevers, convulsions, and headaches (which may be severe),

- Irregular heartbeat and respiration (which may be profound and life-threatening),

- Anxiety and restlessness,

- Excessive repetition of movements and meaningless tasks,

- Formication (the sensation of bugs or worms crawling on or under the skin),

- Psychosis with paranoia, hallucinations, and delusions.

As with any stimulant, psychosis is a common result of Ritalin abuse, and may last for months, even after termination of use.

Chronic users also suffer from anxiety, loss of impulse control, and impaired judgment. The feeling of euphoria or "high" experienced after taking the drug may give way later to severe, suicidal depression. Death by suicide following stimulant use has been reported.

Apart from the direct effects of Ritalin on the body, other complications, specific to the method of intake, occur when the drug is snorted or injected by the user to intensify its effects.

Health Consequences of Snorting Ritalin

Ritalin pills contain the hydrochloride salt methylphenidate. When the salt comes in contact with water, it yields hydrochloric acid. This is not a problem when the pills are taken orally, because hydrochloric acid is one of the digestive acids present in the stomach. When the drug is snorted, however, the corrosive acid can burn the tissues in nasal passages and cause open sores, nosebleeds, and even deterioration of the nasal cartilage.

Health Consequences of Injecting Ritalin

A 100 mg tablet of Ritalin may contain up to 20 mg of the drug. The rest is made up of inert ingredients (lactose, starch, polyethylene glycol, magnesium stearate, sucrose, talc, cellulose, mineral oil, and various dyes and conditioning agents) that are added to make the pill large enough to handle.

All these ingredients, plus other contaminants (such as dust and pollen), are introduced into the body when the user crushes the pill, dissolves it in water, and injects it. Although harmless when taken by mouth, the substances may cause serious problems when injected directly into the veins or body tissues. Apart from the risk of infection by AIDS or hepatitis through the use of contaminated needles, those who inject Ritalin may suffer complications from injection, including

RITALIN ABUSE

Tired of hearing his mother say he was "impossible" without his medicine, and tired of his teacher asking him whether he had forgotten to take his Ritalin whenever he left his seat, Sam gave up. He felt he was lazy, difficult, and obviously stupid, and would never have any friends.

Then, one day, things started to change. He met Dylan, a boy with spiked hair and an earring. Dylan sat beside him on the bus and asked Sam to come to his house to study. Unable to speak, Sam nodded. When Dylan asked him whether he could bring some Ritalin pills with him, Sam agreed.

Going to Dylan's house became a routine for Sam. More and more often, he skipped his medicine and gave it to his new friend. The ironic thing was that Sam's life did not seem to fall apart because he was not taking the pill. His mother continued to complain about his inability to remember his tasks, and his teacher continued to get angry with him for not finishing his work, but that was nothing new for Sam.

One month later, Dylan invited Sam to a party. When Dylan asked him to bring all the Ritalin pills he had at home, Sam did not hesitate. Obviously, Sam did not need them, and Dylan kept telling him how much they helped him study. Sam never questioned whether this were true.

Only as he stood in front of the medicine cabinet that evening, holding the bottle of Ritalin in his hand, did the thought occur to Sam that his mother might notice the pills were gone. He shrugged and put the pills in his jeans pocket anyway. He would just have to come up with an explanation for the pills' disappearance.

blood clots; other infections (such as "blood poisoning" and abscesses); pulmonary problems, including permanent and irreversible lung tissue damage; and skin and circulatory problems.

The hypodermic syringe delivers a concentrated dose of a drug quickly and efficiently, by bypassing many of the body's natural defense mechanisms, such as skin, respiratory cilia, and digestive acids. This rapid delivery makes it difficult to control the intensity of the drug's effects and increases the risk of toxic overdoses.

EFFECTS OF RITALIN ABUSE: ADDICTION

When used regularly, Ritalin produces tolerance, psychological dependence, and withdrawal symptoms—the three characteristics that define addiction. As with other stimulants, Ritalin addiction is particularly rapid. In fact, individuals who abuse stimulants may become addicted in a much shorter period of time than abusers of alcohol or sedative drugs.

"Like amphetamines and cocaine," the DEA warns, "abuse of methylphenidate can lead to marked tolerance and psychic dependence. The pattern of abuse is characterized by escalation of dose, frequent episodes of binge use followed by severe depression, and an overpowering desire to continue the use of this drug despite medical and social consequences."[27]

Tolerance means that constant exposure to a drug produces a reduction of the drug's effect because the brain compensates for the extra stimuli. As a result, the user requires a larger dose to achieve the same effect.

At the same time, in the case of stimulants, some brain functions seem to become more sensitive to stimulation. This may be why Ritalin can cause seizures, cardiac arrhythmias, and psychotic symptoms, such as hallucinations and delusions. When this occurs in children who are taking Ritalin under a doctor's prescription, it can be rather confusing to the parents. They see the drug having less effect on the symptoms that it is supposed to control, instead creating additional and potentially serious, adverse effects.

A person who has been using stimulants experiences a craving for the drug and withdrawal symptoms as soon as the effects of the drug wear off. For Ritalin, this craving can begin as early as a few hours after the last dose. The craving for stimulants occurs in two phases: a "crashing" phase immediately after stopping the drug and a more persistent phase that lasts for a longer period afterward.

The symptoms of Ritalin and amphetamine withdrawal can include psychosis, depression, exhaustion, withdrawal, irritability, suicidal feelings, excitability, euphoria, and hyperactivity.

WONDER DRUGS HOLD THE SEED FOR ADDICTION

Stimulants are uppers. They energize people, allowing them to forget the need for sleep and food. They also increase accuracy and concentration and can make the user feel superhuman.

More than a century ago, the great fictional detective Sherlock Holmes used cocaine to sharpen his mind. Not even he could escape without paying a price, however, and, over the course of four novels, the reader witnesses his fall into addiction. One quote is very appropriate. Holmes's partner, Watson, in *The Sign of Four*, counsels Holmes: "But consider! Count the cost! Your brain may, as you say, be roused and excited, but it is a pathological and morbid process, which involves increased tissue change, and may at least leave a permanent weakness. You know, too, what a black reaction comes upon you. Surely the game is hardly worth the candle. Why should you, for a mere passing pleasure, risk the loss of those great powers with which you have been endowed?"

This is a question that everyone taking stimulants should ponder.

These symptoms may also occur in children who are using Ritalin for the treatment of ADHD. Because some of these symptoms may be the reason the child was put on medication in the first place, parents may not recognize them as a withdrawal reaction. Instead, they may think the child needs another dose of medication or an increase in dosage to treat the underlying symptoms.

Withdrawal from stimulants is not life-threatening physically, but it can be psychologically so if it results in continued depression, suicide, or paranoid or psychotic reactions. Although the withdrawal symptoms caused by stopping the use of a stimulant are less severe than those caused by giving up alcohol or opiates, it is now generally accepted that stimulants do produce an intense craving that is not merely a psychological need.

Usually, children who have been taking Ritalin in low doses under prescription can stop its use without severe consequences. Sometimes, they experience typical withdrawal symptoms. When children are taken off Ritalin, it is better to reduce the dose gradually and under medical supervision. Even if the child has stopped taking the drug abruptly without problems in the past, there is no guarantee that he or she will not have withdrawal symptoms at a later time.

The main danger in a rapid withdrawal is "crashing," which can bring on various mental disturbances, such as fatigue or inertia, depression, and suicidal tendencies. Children also may experience an increased need for food or sleep, and, although it is rare, they may become paranoid and psychotic. The child's behavioral problems are likely to worsen during withdrawal because of the rebound effect of the drug or because of the resurfacing of problems that were masked by it.

With older children, the risk exists that they will turn to other drugs, legal or illegal, to ease the symptoms of withdrawal, so supervision and support during this time is highly recommended.

RITALIN: A GATEWAY TO
ADDICTION AND DRUG ABUSE?

If cocaine is a dangerous and addictive drug, and Ritalin is pharmacologically similar to cocaine, then, theoretically, millions of ADHD children and adults taking Ritalin could be at risk of becoming addicted to the drug. Although no one knows whether this possibility is certain, according to the DEA, "a number of recent studies, drug abuse cases, and trends among adolescents from various sources, indicate that methylphenidate use may be a risk factor for substance abuse." [28] In fact, some studies show that stimulants sensitize the brain to other stimulants, which means that if an individual has been previously exposed to cocaine, amphetamines, or Ritalin, the person will obtain a greater effect upon subsequent exposure to any of them.

Despite this evidence, most Ritalin advocates deny the drug's potential for abuse. For example, Russell Barkley, the author of *Taking Charge of ADHD*, states, "No, Ritalin is not addictive—when taken orally. For this drug to be potentially addictive, it has to be crushed and inhaled nasally, or injected, and that has to be done repeatedly." He also claims that there is "no risk of addiction" when the drug is "taken orally as prescribed." [29]

According to Peter R. Breggins in his book *Talking Back to Ritalin*, both of these last two statements of Barkley's are incorrect. All stimulants are known to be addictive even when taken orally, Breggins contends. Although severe addiction requires a progressive increase in the amount of drug taken, the initial steps toward addiction may begin when the medicine is used by prescription.

Yet most children do not become addicted to Ritalin. In fact, many children do not like taking the drug and stop using it by the time they are 12 or 13 years old. One explanation for this apparent contradiction may be that, even though addiction can start by taking the pill orally, this route is not the ideal way for addiction to develop. Although snorting and injecting produces a quick cocaine-like buzz, taking the drug orally does not produce the same effect. Therefore, it may not lead to the same degree of addiction seen with individuals who use those methods.

Another explanation, according to psychologist Stanton Peele in his book *The Meaning of Addiction,* could be that the mind-altering effects of a drug depend as much on the person who uses it and the context of use as it does on the chemistry of the drug. According to Peele's studies, as indicated in Richard DeGrandpre's *Ritalin Nation,* "a variety of cultural, social, and psychological factors comes together to create the overall drug experience, thus determining whether or not an activity will come to dominate a person's life."[30] Children who take Ritalin by prescription use it in a medical context for what they have been told is a medical problem. Thus, they do not experience the same psychological effects from Ritalin as a recreational user would, because the expectations and reasons for using the drug are different.

Even if children on Ritalin do not become addicted to it in the manner that a recreational user might, Ritalin's use as a medication increases the likelihood of abuse in two ways. Having it available increases the possibility of abuse. Between 2 and 4 million children and 1 million adults nationwide are prescribed Ritalin legally. A May 2000 article in the *Boston Herald* discussed Ritalin's prevalence. "We have a lot of availability, and we have a lot of kids who are aware of what this drug will do to them," stated Gretchen Feussner, a pharmacologist with the DEA. "When you have that combination without much oversight, you are going to have what I think is pretty indiscriminate use of it."[31]

Besides being easy to obtain, Ritalin is also cheaper than other drugs and carries a decreased risk of criminal charges. According to the DEA, illicit prices for a 20-milligram tablet can range from $2 to $20, depending on geographic location. Gretchen Feussner also believes illicit use of Ritalin is even higher on college campuses because parents of Ritalin users are no longer present to supervise their children.[32]

The second, subtler way in which the widespread use of Ritalin may increase abuse is by changing children's overall view of drugs. The fact that Ritalin is so widely used as a medication could make children believe that taking it in other contexts is normal and acceptable as well. When the same drug is used both as medication and as a drug of abuse, the distinction between "good drugs" (drugs used under a doctor's prescription) and "bad drugs" (illegal, addictive drugs) becomes unclear. It may be hard for children to believe that the same drug they are given by their doctor can become dangerous when given, stolen, or sold and used for recreational purposes. And if powerful drugs are seen as being as harmless as vitamins, children may lose the capacity to see a clear difference between appropriate and inappropriate use.

The ease with which the children are prescribed psychotropic drugs may greatly undermine the antidrug messages they receive from school and society. Sometimes, death is the tragic consequence of this confusion. When a teenager died after taking Ritalin and drinking beer at a party in Roanoke, Virginia, in 1995, his friends were surprised to learn that Ritalin was the cause of his death. They did not know that the drug could be fatal. Students have been warned about dangerous drugs, but not about Ritalin. Even if they had been warned, it may have been difficult for them to believe the warning. How could the pill that their little brother takes daily be a dangerous, lethal drug?

TRENDS IN RITALIN ABUSE

Although cases of adults abusing Ritalin have been reported, including examples of teachers and nurses stealing Ritalin

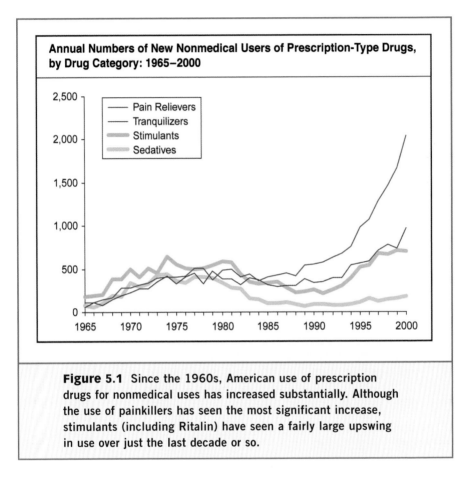

Annual Numbers of New Nonmedical Users of Prescription-Type Drugs, by Drug Category: 1965–2000

- —— Pain Relievers
- —— Tranquilizers
- ▬▬ Stimulants
- ▬▬ Sedatives

Figure 5.1 Since the 1960s, American use of prescription drugs for nonmedical uses has increased substantially. Although the use of painkillers has seen the most significant increase, stimulants (including Ritalin) have seen a fairly large upswing in use over just the last decade or so.

from the school for private use, the most common abusers of stimulants are college and high school students. How many adolescents are abusing Ritalin is unknown, but the available data seem to indicate that the number increased during the 1990s in association with the increased availability of the drug (Figure 5.1).

According to the University of Michigan's annual "Monitoring the Future" study, which surveys drug use in teenagers, the percentage of high school seniors who reported using Ritalin without a doctor's order within the last year grew steadily from 0.3% in 1988 to 2.8% in 1998. In 1990, there were an

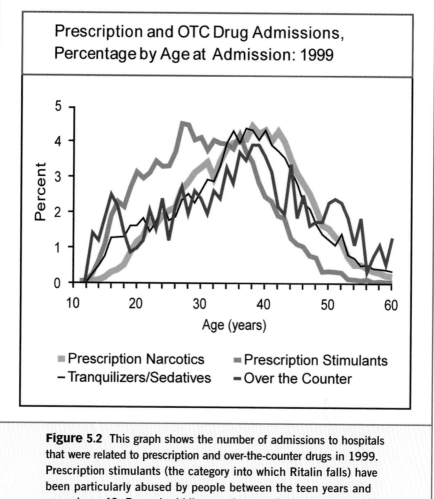

Prescription and OTC Drug Admissions,
Percentage by Age at Admission: 1999

■ Prescription Narcotics   ■ Prescription Stimulants
– Tranquilizers/Sedatives   ■ Over the Counter

Figure 5.2 This graph shows the number of admissions to hospitals that were related to prescription and over-the-counter drugs in 1999. Prescription stimulants (the category into which Ritalin falls) have been particularly abused by people between the teen years and around age 40. Beyond middle age, the use of stimulants falls off dramatically, which highlights the fact that abuse of drugs like Ritalin is especially common—and dangerous—in young adults.

estimated 271 emergency room mentions of Ritalin, according to the Drug Abuse Warning Network (DAWN). In 1998, there were 1,727 incidents, of which about 56% were for children age 10 to 17 (Figure 5.2). A 1996 DEA survey of three states (Wisconsin, South Carolina, and Indiana) found that about

Abusing stimulants

Health officials are concerned with a trend of young people misusing stimulants that are used to treat attention deficit disorder. A survey of students, ages 11 to 18, suggest that many young people seek to obtain ADD medication without a prescription.

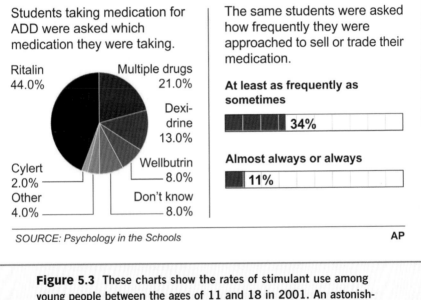

Students taking medication for ADD were asked which medication they were taking.

Ritalin 44.0%
Multiple drugs 21.0%
Dexi-drine 13.0%
Cylert 2.0%
Wellbutrin 8.0%
Other 4.0%
Don't know 8.0%

The same students were asked how frequently they were approached to sell or trade their medication.

At least as frequently as sometimes

34%

Almost always or always

11%

SOURCE: Psychology in the Schools

AP

Figure 5.3 These charts show the rates of stimulant use among young people between the ages of 11 and 18 in 2001. An astonishing 34% of students being treated for ADHD reported being asked to sell their medication for recreational use.

30 to 50% of adolescents in treatment centers were reporting "nonmedical" use of methylphenidate, although it was not identified as their primary drug of abuse. Finally, a 1998 Indiana University survey of 44,232 students found that nearly 7% of high school students surveyed reported using Ritalin illicitly at least once and 2.5% reported using it monthly or more often (Figure 5.3).

Since 2000, however, despite the increased availability of Ritalin, the abuse of it and the consequences of that abuse appear to be declining. Emergency room mentions for Ritalin reported to DAWN declined between 2000 (1,487) and 2001 (1,279).

It should be mentioned that, although Ritalin is the prescription drug most abused by college students, its abuse is still rare compared to drugs such as marijuana or Ecstasy. "I wouldn't even call it a trend," says Judy Phalen, program director for alcohol and drug education at Northeastern University in an article in the *Boston Herald*. "It's fairly random and sporadic." As a 1998 Boston University graduate put it, "I know a lot of kids that are on Ritalin normally. And their roommates would get some (from them) and snort it or whatever to study, but it wasn't too prevalent. Most people just smoke pot." John Knight of Children's Hospital agrees: "I've heard reports back from kids who have had their (Ritalin) stolen when they go away to college, so it does happen. But it's not common."[33]

RITALIN ABUSE: THE REAL PARADOX

Ritalin works. It makes children concentrate and behave, calms them down, and makes them easier to handle. So, detractors claim, would cocaine, if it were given in the same context. Laboratory experiments show that rats able to self-administer cocaine do so repeatedly, choosing the drug over food and sex until they die. They do the same with Ritalin.

Because Ritalin has virtually the same pharmacological properties as cocaine, the real paradox about the extensive use of Ritalin in ADHD children seems to be not that Ritalin calms them down, but that they do not become addicted to it.

Although addiction in children who take low-dose Ritalin pills orally and in a medical context is not common, this does not mean that Ritalin cannot be abused. Of all prescription drugs, Ritalin is the first choice of abuse on college campuses. Its availability, low price, and familiarity may contribute to its popularity.

6

Ritalin in the United States

COSMETIC USE OF RITALIN: THE SEARCH FOR PERFECTION

Children take it under doctors' orders to stop fidgeting and pay attention. College students snort it to get high or cram for finals. In one case, Ritalin is considered a prescription drug, and its use is medically sanctioned. In the other, it is called a drug of abuse, and its use is a felony. However, the distinction between use and abuse is not always clear.

Sometimes, the person taking Ritalin without a prescription is a teenager whose intelligence is above average but whose grades are not, and who thinks Ritalin will improve his or her motivation, concentration, and, consequently, grades. Or maybe it is an adult who takes Ritalin to control his or her difficult personality to relate better to other people at work and in personal life. Perhaps it a baseball player who may use Ritalin to help him keep more focused on the game and improve his performance. Ritalin is sometimes given to children by parents and teachers to solve behavioral problems that they do not have the time to solve. Other parents may see Ritalin's positive short-term effects in performance as a way of giving their children a competitive edge at school, because they are better able to focus and concentrate.

In all these cases, Ritalin is used not as a treatment for a real disorder, but rather as a way to manage and improve behavior. It

RITALIN: COSMETIC USE

Leslie had struggled in school all her life. She was obviously smart, but her performance was somewhat lacking. Mainly, she had trouble completing assignments. She was able to start them, but then she would lose interest and move on to the next project, leaving the first one unfinished.

Still, Leslie had managed to get As and Bs most of the time, which was fine with her. It would have been fine, that is, if her parents had not decided before she had even been born that she was going to be a lawyer.

With the SAT exams only months away, the pressure to buckle down and concentrate harder increased, and Leslie panicked. She feared she would not do well, and when her mother suggested that Ritalin might help her overcome what she called "her laziness," Leslie agreed to see an ADHD specialist.

The doctor hesitated. If the severity were stretched a little, Leslie's symptoms could qualify her for an ADHD diagnosis. Yet she was not really handicapped by the symptoms, since she was getting good grades and her social life was normal.

Leslie's mother was not going to be deterred by a technicality. "If Ritalin can help Leslie in her studies," she asked, "what is wrong with taking it?"

The doctor gave in and prescribed Ritalin. Leslie got straight As that year and a great SAT score, but she was not happy. She complained that Ritalin made her irritable and that her social life had suffered from it. Eventually, her dose of Ritalin had to be increased to keep her concentration up, and the side effects became worse. Leslie started questioning whether she really wanted to go to college. She felt she could not go to school without Ritalin, but she did not want to take Ritalin forever.

Leslie and her parents argued. Finally, they reached a compromise. She could stop taking Ritalin, but she would go to college for a full year before deciding whether she really wanted to give up.

is for this and similar uses of a drug that Peter Kramer, in his book *Listening to Prozac,* coined the expression "cosmetic pharmacology." Whether it is all right to use Ritalin for enhancement is a controversial issue in academic and athletic settings. The United States and International Olympic committees have banned Ritalin from their competitions. But professional and collegiate organizations, such as the National Basketball Association (NBA) and the National Collegiate Athletic Association (NCAA), accept its use as a "medication," dismissing its possible performance-enhancing effects. In the academic setting, taking Ritalin is allowed during the SAT exams and in national entrance exams for graduate and law school. Some medical practitioners, such as Joseph Biederman, see no problem with using Ritalin as an enhancement. "It's like wearing glasses to achieve 20/20 vision," Biederman says. "If inattention or distractibility is preventing optimum performance, why not give Ritalin?"[34] The alternative, he thinks, would be similar to letting a child squint to correct a fundamental defect in vision.

On the other hand, Diller is not convinced by this argument. The standards for good vision are much more precise and objective than those for good behavior or performance, he reasons, and the measures for 20/20 vision are clearly defined, while there is no standardized test or biological marker for behavior. Diller is uneasy about the idea of giving "medication for a condition whose chief trait is the failure to perform up to one's potential—or to manage one's life efficiently." Although he agrees that there is nothing wrong per se with wanting to enhance human potential, he believes that giving Ritalin to students who would perform adequately without it would lessen their achievement.[35]

Not everyone agrees. For instance, the organization Children and Adults with Attention Deficit Disorder (CHADD) strongly argues for Ritalin use as a way to improve performance, as the following paragraph, which appeared in the organization's national magazine, *Attention!*, shows:

> Consider a college student who achieves at an above-average level overall. Specifically, suppose that, due to dyslexia and ADD, his reading speed is 50 percent of the average student's reading speed. Suppose further that he spends twice as much time as his classmates on reading assignments. Does his extraordinary effort, resulting in overall above-average performance, mean that he should not be permitted accommodations (e.g., books on tape) for his reading difficulty? And Ritalin for his ADD? [31]

This argument, which can be summarized by the slogan "It works, so why not use it?" has been repeatedly used by Ritalin advocates.

Ritalin detractors do not agree. Although Ritalin has an immediate effect in making children calmer, they argue, that does not mean that Ritalin solves their problems. On the contrary, some studies show that it actually dims cognitive abilities. Opponents say that children on Ritalin are not quieter because they are involved in learning; they are just quiet. Furthermore, there is no evidence of any long-term benefit for academic performance, psychological well-being, or pro-social behavior in a child who takes Ritalin. In fact, studies suggest that giving Ritalin to children undermines their psychological development, leaving them dependent on the daily intake of a mind-altering drug.

RITALIN AND THE DRUG ENFORCEMENT ADMINISTRATION

Since 1971, the DEA, the agency responsible for the regulation and control of substances with potential for abuse, has classified Ritalin in the Schedule II category of drugs, together with cocaine, amphetamines, methamphetamine (speed), and morphine. These are drugs with a medical use that have the highest abuse potential and dependence profile. As a substance in Schedule II, Ritalin's production and distribution are tightly regulated, and dealing in or distributing Ritalin is a serious felony under both federal and state laws.

The organization CHADD does not believe that Ritalin is a dangerous substance. On the contrary, it is CHADD's philosophy that the symptoms of hyperactivity and inattention generally known as ADHD have a neurobiological cause—a chemical imbalance in the brain—that Ritalin, a mild stimulant that has no health risk for the user, corrects. Many, if not most, parents of children with ADHD accept this philosophy, and, in the 1990s, when the number of Ritalin prescriptions increased dramatically and there were rumors of a Ritalin shortage, they started to question the wisdom of the DEA's classification. Why should Ritalin, a harmless medicine prescribed to their children by a physician, be a Schedule II substance? Why should there be a quota for its production? Why should they have to pay to go to the doctor every month to get a written prescription for it?

In October 1993, Ciba-Geigy, then the pharmaceutical manufacturer of Ritalin, sent letters to physicians announcing the possibility of a Ritalin shortage (due, the company claimed, to a delay at the DEA in approving the production quota for the year). Regardless of the fact that few, if any, parents had problems obtaining the drug, this letter prompted CHADD and the American Academy of Neurology to write a petition to the DEA, asking the agency to remove Ritalin from the Schedule II list.

Upon receiving the petition, the DEA started a thorough investigation that involved national and international experts in fields as varied as ADHD research and treatment, psychiatry, social work, ethics, and law enforcement. The results of the DEA investigation did not support CHADD's contention that

Ritalin is a mild stimulant. On the contrary, the studies found that Ritalin, although effective in treating the symptoms of ADHD, shows no clear long-term improvement on users and can have dangerous effects on health, including death. Because the effects of Ritalin on humans are virtually identical to those produced by cocaine, amphetamine, and methamphetamine (speed), the researchers noted that its abuse liability is high and can lead to marked tolerance and psychological dependence.

Although cases of adults and adolescents abusing their prescribed Ritalin have been reported, most people who abuse Ritalin get the drug illegally. Unlike other drugs of abuse, such as cocaine or methamphetamine, which are manufactured illegally, the Ritalin available for abuse comes from diversion of the pharmaceutical product. Diversion of Ritalin is done through prescription forgery (i.e., physicians forging Ritalin prescriptions for their own use or for sale), "attention deficit scams" (in which parents take their children to different physicians to obtain the drug for use, sale, or trade), illegal sales, or drug thefts. Break-ins, armed robbery, and employee theft all have been reported in pharmacies. According to DEA records: [37]

- From January 1990 to May 1995, methylphenidate ranked in the top 10 most frequently reported controlled drugs stolen from registrants.

- From January 1996 to December 1997, about 700,000 dosage units of methylphenidate were reported to the drug theft database.

- In 1998, there were 376 reported thefts of methylphenidate from pharmacies.

In addition, Ritalin has also been stolen from schools and homes. This is especially significant because, unlike pharmacies that are required by state and federal laws to keep a record of the Ritalin they handle, schools do not have such a requirement. In fact, most schools do not know how much Ritalin they have at a certain time and usually keep it unlocked. A 1996 DEA survey found that most schools did not have a nurse dispensing medication. This task was left up to school secretaries, parent aides, teachers, or, in one case, a janitor. Under these circumstances, it is no surprise that schools are an easy target for drug theft.

Moreover, information from DEA case files and state investigative services show that Ritalin is involved in criminal drug-trafficking activities, including: [38]

- Street sales as determined by undercover buys,

- Multistate distribution rings,

- Multidrug distribution rings (with cocaine, LSD, marijuana, hydromorphone, diazepam, and anabolic steroids),

- Smuggling from Mexico.

Because the magnitude and significance of these diversion and trafficking activities are comparable to those of pharmaceutical drugs of similar abuse potential and availability, the DEA believes that "There is little doubt Schedule II controls and the lack of clandestine production have limited the illegal use of the drug." [39]

As the DEA was taking the usual steps to prepare its preliminary response, in which it planned to deny CHADD's petition, the Merrow Report (a team of journalists) produced a television documentary on the ADHD-Ritalin epidemic. When it aired on PBS in October 1995, the documentary revealed a connection between Ritalin's manufacturer—then Ciba-Geigy, now Novartis—and CHADD. Ciba-Geigy had contributed nearly $900,000 to CHADD over five years, a fact that raised concerns about whether CHADD's agenda had been influenced by the pharmaceutical company. The United Nations International Narcotics Control Board questioned whether a money transfer from a pharmaceutical company to promote sales of an internationally controlled substance could be viewed as hidden advertising. If this were the case, it would violate the provisions of a 1971 narcotics control treaty that the United States had signed. Whether due to the discovery of this connection or for other reasons, in early 1996, CHADD withdrew its petition asking the DEA to take Ritalin off the Schedule II list.

Currently, Ritalin remains a Schedule II substance, because the DEA believes "continued increases in the medical prescription of these drugs without the appropriate safeguards to ensure medication compliance and accountability can only lead to increased stimulant abuse among U.S. children."[40]

RITALIN: WHO BENEFITS?

If Ritalin is such a dangerous drug, then why has it become so widely used in the United States? Why are so many doctors prescribing it? Why are so many parents and teachers asking for Ritalin prescriptions for children?

A possible answer to these questions is that many people do not know that Ritalin is dangerous, believing instead that it is a valuable and indispensable medicine. They believe what pharmaceutical companies and organizations such as CHADD tell them—that ADHD has a biological cause and that Ritalin is a benign, mild substance that can cure ADHD.

Both affirmations are false. Ritalin is not a safe drug. As the DEA puts it, "There is an abundance of scientific literature that indicates that methylphenidate shares the same abuse potential as other Schedule II stimulants."[41] As we have seen in Chapter 3, despite widespread belief to the contrary, there is no proof that ADHD has a biological cause. Even when informed that a biological cause for ADHD has not been found, most people—

even physicians—continue to believe that a biological cause exists. Richard DeGrandpre, explains the reason for this in his book *Ritalin Nation*:

> Behind this belief are the thousands of practicing psy-chiatrists and pediatricians who rely on the diagnosis, the pharmaceutical companies that make millions of dollars each year from ADHD-drugs, and the hundreds of thousands of families and teachers who seek shelter behind the diagnosis and its so-called treatment [Ritalin].[42]

The reason that pharmaceutical companies would support the view that ADHD has a biological cause seems obvious. A biological cause means that a drug (usually Ritalin) is the treatment of choice, and selling stimulants is a profitable business. The DEA estimates that pharmaceutical companies earn approximately $450 million a year from the sales of stimulants, and nearly all of the stimulants sold legally in the United States are prescribed for ADHD treatment.

Pharmaceutical companies also spend a lot of money marketing their products, either directly to the public by advertising or indirectly through physicians or through the support of national ADHD organizations like CHADD. Direct advertising increases sales by making the public aware of the drug in a positive light (most people do not read the small print where the side effects are listed) and by giving the drug an aura of scientific approval and safety.

It was thanks to money from Ciba-Geigy that CHADD grew to 600 chapters and 35,000 members nationwide by 1993. CHADD provides useful information and a support network for adults with ADHD or families raising children with ADHD-related problems. Yet its strong belief in the neurobiological cause for ADHD and its slant toward the use of Ritalin as the main form of treatment makes those who do not share these opinions feel unwelcome. CHADD's former connection to Ciba-Geigy has made some people question the organization's objectivity. CHADD denies that this relationship influenced any of its policies or pronouncements concerning medication. It justified accepting money from Ciba-Geigy because, otherwise, it "would not be able to conduct important educational activities."[43] Pharmaceutical companies also understand the importance of advertising their products to physicians. Many physicians get their information about new drugs from these advertisements. Physicians are also the ultimate distributors of pharmaceutical products, and advertising may sway their decision on what type of medication to prescribe.

In the case of Ritalin, physicians also have a pragmatic reason for choosing the drug over more time-consuming treatments, such as individual or family therapy. In today's system of managed care, physicians can lose money if they spend too much time with particular patients or give referrals for specialists. In this situation, Ritalin seems to be the perfect solution, and because Ritalin has a quick effect on disruptive children, parents and teachers tend to agree.

POSSIBLE REASONS FOR THE INCREASE IN THE INCIDENCE OF ADHD AND RITALIN USE IN THE UNITED STATES

As stated in Chapter 4, the number of children and adults diagnosed with ADHD in the United States has risen from 900,000 in 1990 to about 5 million in 2000.[44] The reason for this steep increase is not clear. Some authors argue that there has been no actual increase in the number of cases, but a change in the environment, in the culture where children grow up. This change in the culture draws attention to symptoms (now called ADHD) that, in a more primitive society, would have gone undetected, because they would not have been viewed as negative. In fact, they may have been an asset. For instance, in a hunting society, being able to be constantly on the move and eager to take on new challenges would have been a valuable trait. Also, in the past, children who did not do well in school could drop out to work on the family farm or join the military. It was only when education became mandatory in the 20th century, and all children had to sit for hours at a desk, that the symptoms of ADHD became a liability.

Other authors believe the rise in the number of children with ADHD-like symptoms is real. Richard DeGrandpre, for instance, believes it is a consequence of the increased speed of modern life. Children growing up in the United States today are exposed from a very early age to television, computers, and video games. Used to this constant stimulation, their minds demand a high level of stimuli. When this need is not met—for instance, when they must concentrate on some not-so-exciting task in the classroom—children get bored and fidget or try to keep up the stimuli level through other means. According to this theory, Ritalin, a stimulant itself, provides the mind with an internal stimulus, and, consequently, the child does not need to move or talk to look for an external one.

But this cannot be the only reason for the rise in U.S. cases. After all, this increase in external stimuli has also happened in Europe or Japan, yet the number of ADHD cases has not increased so dramatically in those places.

So why has there been such an increase only in the United States? Some blame it on the American ancestors. Immigrants, from whom most Americans descend, are by definition an adventurous and rootless kind of people, always on the move, and these are exactly the traits that people with ADHD have. However, most sociobiologists do not agree. They believe that 400 years of a separate history is too short a time to produce a distinct evolutionary difference.

Others blame the Declaration of Independence. Because the "pursuit of happiness" is a fundamental American goal, American expectations are higher than those of people in other countries. Americans do not accept imperfection, disappointment, or discomfort easily. If they are in pain, they take painkillers; if depressed, they take antidepressants. If a child is difficult or is not getting ahead at school, why shouldn't a drug fix that, too? (Figure 6.1)

For Diller, this difference in the incidence of ADHD between the United States and other countries might be due to what he calls the "politically correct parenting" popular in the contemporary United States. Until recently, parents would discipline their children by following the old adage "Spare the rod, spoil the child." Today, parents in other

RITALIN AND THE FREEDOM OF CHOICE

Children come with all sorts of personalities and with different sets of skills. Because American society praises financial success over just about anything else, American parents push their children toward those careers believed to be most lucrative—careers that usually require going to college. This results in an emphasis on academics and the competition for grades, and the need for a pill to help those who are not naturally inclined toward this goal.

But is drugging the child good for the child, or for society as a whole? Wouldn't it be better to change the expectations and let children choose their own goals?

After all, in retrospect, no one would think it would have been a good idea to force the Beatles to work as bookkeepers, Luciano Pavarotti to play basketball, or Britney Spears to become a heart surgeon. And all these people were or are successful, exactly because they did or are doing what they like best.

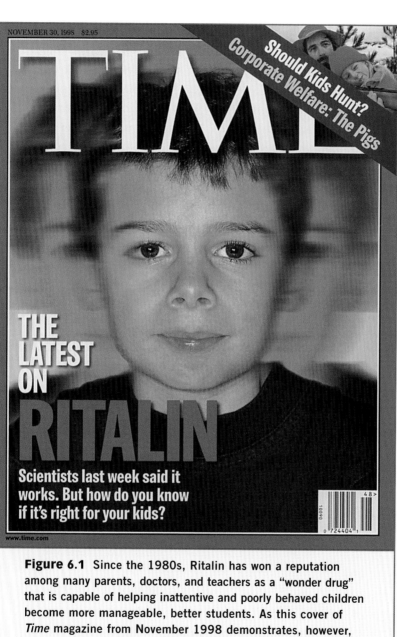

NOVEMBER 30, 1998 $2.95

TIME

Corporate Welfare: The Pigs
Should Kids Hunt?

THE LATEST ON RITALIN

Scientists last week said it works. But how do you know if it's right for your kids?

www.time.com

Figure 6.1 Since the 1980s, Ritalin has won a reputation among many parents, doctors, and teachers as a "wonder drug" that is capable of helping inattentive and poorly behaved children become more manageable, better students. As this cover of *Time* magazine from November 1998 demonstrates, however, some experts question whether Ritalin should be used so frequently, and whether it is right for every child who shows symptoms similar to those of ADHD.

cultures still spank or otherwise physically punish children, while parents in the United States often believe such punishment is wrong and are reluctant to use it. With the change in punishment techniques, ADHD symptoms have become more apparent in children. Physical punishment, however, does not solve the problem, either. Children may seem to comply in the short term, but eventually, they will likely show their anger in unpredictable ways.

Another factor in the ADHD/Ritalin boom in the United States may be the disintegration of the family and the pressure of working in the corporate environment. The American family has changed dramatically over the last few decades. It is no longer composed of two parents and children with a close extended family nearby for support. Today, the nuclear family has shrunk to two parents and the children or to one parent and the children. The extended family now often refers to remarried parents, each of whom brings his or her own children to the mixture. This type of extended family, with so many conflicting needs as part of its very nature, may not be the ideal situation for giving individual attention to every child.

In most American families, both parents now work, or, in the case of single-parent families, the one parent must work to support the family. In either case, the demands of a job mean that there is no one home with the sole responsibility for taking care of the children, as was usually the case in previous generations. Babies are forced to wake up early to be brought to day care when they are barely one month old. This fixed schedule is stressful to all children, and, although most adapt, some do not. When the stress shows in these children as crankiness or troublemaking, the search for the cause of this "maladaptive" behavior starts. Parents are told that the child has separation anxiety disorder, sensory integration disorder, or ADHD, but—they are often reassured—this is not their fault; there is a neurophysiological cause for this behavior. Eventually, the children may be given Ritalin.

For a short period of time, the behavioral problems may seem to be solved. However, these seemingly beneficial effects need to be balanced against the fact that:

- Ritalin is a dangerous drug,

- Ritalin has no effect on long-term performance,

- 3.5 million children in the United States are taking Ritalin today,

- The United States consumes 85% of the entire world's Ritalin.

Is Ritalin really the best solution in the long run? Peter R. Breggin does not think so. As he writes in his book *Talking Back to Ritalin*:

> The drugging of children for behavior control should raise profound spiritual, philosophical, and ethical questions about ourselves as adults and about how we view the children in our care. Society ignores these critical questions at great peril to itself, to its values, and to the well-being of its children.[45]

Lack of attention, overworked parents, and the disappointment that follows when high expectations are not met may all be factors that contribute to the increased number of American children on Ritalin. Because, in the short term, Ritalin seems to work, and because behavioral approaches are often time-consuming, it tends to be easier for parents, teachers, and doctors to turn to Ritalin as a solution than to employ nonpharmacological treatments for the children in their care.

When children are given Ritalin instead of being taught ways to deal with their difficulties, however, what they learn is that drugs are the answer to emotional problems. This may prove to be a very dangerous belief to bring with them into their teen and adult years.

Notes

1. Walker III, Sydney. *The Hyperactivity Hoax. How to Stop Drugging Your Child and Find Real Medical Help.* New York: St. Martin's Press, 1998, p. 249.

2. Bradley, Charles. "The Behavior of Children Receiving Benzedrine." *American Journal of Psychiatry* 94 (1937): 577–585.

3. Statistics available online at *http://www.dea.gov.*

4. Diller, Lawrence H. *Running on Ritalin. A Physician Reflects on Children, Society, and Performance in a Pill.* New York: Bantam Books, 1988, p. 25.

5. The Merrow Report. Available online at *http://www.pbs.org/ merrow/tv/add/index.html.*

6. Walker, p. 6.

7. Diller, p. 74.

8. DeGrandpre, Richard. *Ritalin Nation.* New York: W.W. Norton, 1999, p. 174.

9. Diller, p. 74.

10. Ibid., p. 42.

11. Zametkin, Alan J., et al. "Cerebral Glucose Metabolism in Adults with Hyperactivity of Childhood Onset." *New England Journal of Medicine* 323 (1990): 1361–1366.

12. Elmer-De Witt, P. "Why Junior Won't Sit Still: Researchers Link Hyperactivity to an Abnormality in the Brain." *Time.* November 26, 1990.

13. Zametkin, A., as quoted in Breggin, Peter R. *Talking Back to Ritalin.* Monroe, ME: Common Courage Press, 1998, p. 169.

14. *Philadelphia Inquirer* magazine, March 16, 2003, p. 11.

15. Breggin, p. 169.

16. Carlson E. A., D. Jacobvitz, and L. A. Sroufe. "A Developmental Investigation of Inattentiveness and Hyperactivity." *Child Development* 66 (1995): 37–54.

17. Diller, p. 6.

18. Hallowell, Edward M., and John J. Ratey. *Driven to Distraction: Recognizing and Coping with Attention Deficit Disorder from Childhood Through Adulthood.* New York: Pantheon Books, 1994.

19. Hallowell, Edward M. "What I've learned from ADD." *Psychology Today.* May/June 1997, pp. 40–44.

20. Harmann, Thom. *Attention Deficit Disorder: A Different Perception.* Grass Valley, CA: Underwood Books, 1993.

21. Hallowell and Ratey, p. 209.

22. Diller, p. 2.

23. Maurer, Katherine. "African-American Children Less Likely to Get Ritalin." *Clinical Psychiatry News* 24 (1996): 1–2.

24. DeGrandpre, p. 175.

25. Breggin, pp. 72–73.

26. Bailey, William J., M.P.H., C.P.P. Indiana Prevention Resource Center. The Clearinghouse Fact Series. The Trustees of Indiana University, 1995.

27. Report available online at *http://www.dea.gov/pubs/ congrtest/ct051500.htm.*

28. Terrance Woodworth, spokesperson for the DEA in the closing statement of his May 16, 2000, testimony before the congressional Committee on Education and the Workforce: Subcommittee on Early Childhood, Youth and Families.

29. Barkley, Russell A. *Taking Charge of ADHD*. New York: The Guilford Press, 1995.

30. DeGrandpre, p. 179.

31. Hanchett, Doug. *Boston Herald*, May 21, 2000. Available online at *http://www.mapinc.org/drugnews/v00.n670.a07.html*.

32. Ibid.

33. Ibid.

34. Diller, p. 298.

35. Ibid., p. 323.

36. Ibid.

37. Woodworth.

38. Ibid.

39. Ibid.

40. Ibid.

41. Ibid.

42. DeGrandpre.

43. An Open Letter to CHADD Available online at *http://netacc.net/~gradda/wi95tele.html*.

44. Swanson J. M., M. Lerner, and W. Lillie. "More Frequent Diagnosis of Attention Deficit-Hyperactivity Disorder." *New England Journal of Medicine* 333 (1996): 994.

45. Breggin, p. 140.

Bibliography

Books

Barkley, Russell A. *Attention Deficit Disorder: A Handbook for Diagnosis and Treatment*. New York: The Guilford Press, 1990.

————. *Taking Charge of ADHD*. New York: The Guilford Press, 1995.

Breggin, Peter R. *Reclaiming Our Children*. Cambridge, MA: Perseus Books, 2000.

————. *Talking Back to Ritalin*. Monroe, ME: Common Courage Press, 1998.

DeGrandpre, Richard. *Ritalin Nation*. New York: W.W. Norton, 1999.

Diller, Lawrence H. *Running on Ritalin. A Physician Reflects on Children, Society, and Performance in a Pill*. New York: Bantam Books, 1988.

Garber, Stephen W., Marianne Daniels Garber, and Robyn Freedman Spizman. *Beyond Ritalin*. New York: Villard, 1996.

Goodsell, David S. *Our Molecular Nature: The Body's Motors, Machines and Messages*. New York: Springer-Verlag, 1996.

Gordon, Michael. *ADHD/Hyperactivity: A Consumer's Guide*. New York: GSI Publications, 1991.

Haber, Julian S. *ADHD: The Great Misdiagnosis*. Dallas: FAAP Taylor Trade Publishing, 2000.

Hallowell, Edward M., and John J. Ratey. *Driven to Distraction: Recognizing and Coping with Attention Deficit Disorder from Childhood Through Adulthood*. New York: Pantheon Books, 1994.

Harmann, Thom. *Attention Deficit Disorder: A Different Perception*. Grass Valley, CA: Underwood Books, 1993.

Hesse, Karen. *The Music of Dolphins*. New York: Scholastic, 1996.

Kramer, Peter D. *Listening to Prozac*. New York: Penguin Books, 1993.

Levinson, Harold N. *Total Concentration: How to Understand Attention Deficit Disorders*. New York: M. Evans and Company, 1990.

Millichap, Gordon J. *Attention Deficit Hyperactivity and Learning Disorders: Questions and Answers*. Chicago: PNB Publishers, 1998.

Peele, Stanton. *The Meaning of Addiction: Compulsive Experience and Its Interpretation*. Lexington, MA: Lexington Books, 1985.

Schrag, Peter, and Diane Divoky. *The Myth of the Hyperactive Child, and Other Means of Child Control*. New York: Pantheon Books, 1975.

Silver, Larry. *Dr. Larry Silver's Advice to Parents on ADHD*, 2nd ed. New York: Random House/Times Books, 1999.

Walker III, Sydney. *The Hyperactivity Hoax. How to Stop Drugging Your Child and Find Real Medical Help*. New York: St. Martin's Press, 1998.

Articles

Biederman, Joseph. "Are Stimulants Overprescribed for Children with Behavioral Problems?" *Pediatric News*. August 1996, p. 26.

Bradley, Charles. "The Behavior of Children Receiving Benzedrine." *American Journal of Psychiatry* 94 (1937): 577–585.

———. "Benzedrine and Dexedrine in the Treatment of Children's Behavior Disorders." *Pediatrics* 5 (1950): 24–37.

Carlson E.A., D. Jacobvitz, and L.A. Sroufe. "A Developmental Investigation of Inattentiveness and Hyperactivity." *Child Development* 66 (1995): 37–54.

Elmer-De Witt, Phil. "Why Junior Won't Sit Still: Researchers Link Hyperactivity to an Abnormality in the Brain." *Time*. November 26, 1990.

Maurer, Katherine. "African-American Children Less Likely to Get Ritalin." *Clinical Psychiatry News* 24 (1996): 1–2.

Rapoport, Judith L., Monte S. Buchsbaum, et al. "Dextroamphetamine: Cognitive and Behavioral Effects in Normal Prepubertal Boys." *Science* 199 (1978): 560–563.

———. "Dextroamphetamine: Its Cognitive and Behavioral Effects in Normal and Hyperactive Boys and Normal Men." *Archives of General Psychiatry* 37 (1980): 933–943.

Swanson, J.M., M. Lerner, and W. Lillie. "More Frequent Diagnosis of Attention Deficit-Hyperactivity Disorder." *New England Journal of Medicine* 333 (1996): 994.

Weiss, Bernard, and Victor G. Laties. "The Enhancement of Human Performance by Caffeine and the Amphetamines." *Pharmacological Review* 14 (1962): 1–36.

Zametkin, Alan J., et al. "Cerebral Glucose Metabolism in Adults with Hyperactivity of Childhood Onset." *New England Journal of Medicine* 323 (1990): 1361–1366.

Zametkin, Alan J., Laura L. Liebenauer, et al. "Brain Metabolism in Teenagers with Attention-Deficit Hyperactivity Disorder." *Archives of General Psychiatry* 50 (1993): 333–340.

Bibliography

Web Sites

ADD/ADHD Statement of Drug Enforcement Administration. Gene R. Haislip, Deputy Assistant Administrator. Office of Diversion Control, Drug Enforcement Administration. United States Department of Justice, Washington, D.C. At the conclusion of the conference on Stimulant Use in the Treatment of ADHD. Available online at *http://www.add-adhd.org/ritalin.html*.

Bailey, William J., M.P.H., C.P.P. "Ritalin Abuse." Clearinghouse Fact Series. The Trustees of Indiana University. Indiana Prevention Resource Center, 1995. Available online at *http://www.drugs.indiana.edu/publications/iprc/factline/ritalin.html?*.

"Banning Ritalin in Colorado." *Dateline*. October 21, 1999. Available online at *http://www.nfgcc.org/banritalin.htm*.

"Methylphenidate (A Background Paper)." Drug and Chemical Evaluation Section Office of Diversion Control, Drug Enforcement Administration, Department of Justice, Washington, D.C., October 1995. Available online at *http://www.bioethics.gov/background/humanflourish.html*.

NIH Consensus Statement on Diagnosis and Treatment of Attention Deficit Hyperactivity Disorder. Available online at *http://consensus.nih.gov*.

"Ritalin Use Among Youth: Examining the Issues and Concerns." Hearing before the Subcommittee on Early Childhood Youth and Families of the Committee on Education and the Workforce." House of Representatives. 106th Congress, Second Session. Hearing held in Washington, D.C., May 16, 2000. Serial No. 106–109. Available online at *http://commdocs.house.gov/committees/edu/hedcew6-109.000/hedcew6-109.htm*.

"Speed Chills-Ritalin Hits Campuses." *Boston Herald*. May 21, 2000. Available online at *http://www.mapinc.org/drugnews/v00.n670.a07.html*.

Terrance Woodworth, Deputy Director. Office of Diversion Control, Drug Enforcement Administration. Testimony before the Congressional Committee on Education and the Workforce: Subcommittee on Early Childhood, Youth and Families. May 16, 2000. Available online at *http://www.dea.gov/pubs/cngrtest/ct051600.htm*.

Further Reading

Barkley, Russell A. *Attention Deficit Disorder: A Handbook for Diagnosis and Treatment*. New York: The Guilford Press, 1990.

———. *Taking Charge of ADHD*. New York: The Guilford Press, 1995.

Beal, Eileen. *Everything You Need to Know About ADD/ADHD*. New York: Rosen Publishing, 1998.

Breggin, Peter R. *Reclaiming Our Children*. Cambridge, MA: Perseus Books, 2000.

———. *Talking Back to Ritalin*. Monroe, ME: Common Courage Press, 1998.

DeGrandpre, Richard. *Ritalin Nation*. New York: W.W. Norton, 1999.

Diller, Lawrence H. *Running on Ritalin: A Physician Reflects on Children, Society, and Performance in a Pill*. New York: Bantam Books, 1988.

Garber, Stephen W., Marianne Daniels Garber, and Robyn Freedman Spizman. *Beyond Ritalin*. New York: Villard, 1996.

Goleman, Daniel. *Emotional Intelligence*. New York: Bantam, 1995.

Gordon, Michael. *ADHD/Hyperactivity: A Consumer's Guide*. New York: GSI Publications, 1991.

Haber, Julian S. *ADHD: The Great Misdiagnosis*. Dallas: FAAP Taylor Trade Publishing, 2000.

Hallowell, Edward M., and John J. Ratey. *Driven to Distraction: Recognizing and Coping with Attention Deficit Disorder from Childhood Through Adulthood*. New York: Pantheon Books, 1994.

Levinson, Harold N. *Total Concentration: How to Understand Attention Deficit Disorders*. New York: M. Evans and Company, 1990.

Millichap, Gordon J. *Attention Deficit Hyperactivity and Learning Disorders: Questions and Answers*. Chicago: PNB Publishers, 1998.

Morrison, Jaydene. *Coping with ADD/ADHD*. New York: Rosen Publishing, 2000.

Silver, Larry. *Dr. Larry Silver's Advice to Parents on ADHD*, 2nd ed. New York: Random House/Times Books, 1999.

Walker III, Sydney. *The Hyperactivity Hoax: How to Stop Drugging Your Child and Find Real Medical Help*. New York: St. Martin's Press, 1998.

Williams, Julie. *Attention Deficit/Hyperactivity Disorder*. Berkeley Heights, NJ: Enslow Publishers, 2001.

Further Reading

Web Sites
Attention Deficit Disorder Association (ADDA)
http://www.add.org

Center for Substance Abuse Prevention (CSAP)
http://preventiion.samhsa.gov

Child Development Institute
http://www.cdipage.com/adhd.htm

Children and Adults with Attention Deficit Disorder (CHADD)
http://www.chadd.org

Dr. Peter Breggin's Web Site. "Ritalin, Adderall, Other Stimulants."
http://www.breggin.com/ritalin.html

Indiana Prevention Resource Center Factline on
    Non-Medical Use of Ritalin
http://www.drugs.indiana.edu/pubs/factline/ritalin.html

Michigan Education Report
http://www.educationreport.org/pubs/mer/article.asp?ID=3218

National Institute of Drug Abuse (NIDA)
http://www.nida.nih.gov/

National Institute of Mental Health
http://www.nida.nih.gov/Infofax/ritalin.html

Ounce of Prevention Fund
http://www.esc-chicago.org/project%20profiles/ounce.htm

Index

Index

Index

Picture Credits

About the Author

A Spanish native, **Carmen Ferreiro**, Ph.D., obtained her doctoral degree in biology from the Universidad Autónoma of Madrid, Spain, and worked as a researcher for over ten years both in Spain and at the University of California, Davis. Apart from the papers originated from her research in the fields of biochemistry and plant virology, she also wrote the book *Heroin* for this series. She now lives in the United States as an independent writer and translator.

About the Editor

David J. Triggle is a University Professor and a Distinguished Professor in the School of Pharmacy and Pharmaceutical Sciences at the State University of New York at Buffalo. He studied in the United Kingdom and earned his B.Sc. degree in Chemistry from the University of Southampton and a Ph.D. degree in Chemistry at the University of Hull. Following post-doctoral work at the University of Ottawa in Canada and the University of London in the United Kingdom, he assumed a position at the School of Pharmacy at Buffalo. He served as Chairman of the Department of Biochemical Pharmacology from 1971 to 1985 and as Dean of the School of Pharmacy from 1985 to 1995. From 1995 to 2001 he served as the Dean of the Graduate School, and as the University Provost from 2000 to 2001. He is the author of several books dealing with the chemical pharmacology of the autonomic nervous system and drug-receptor interactions, some 400 scientific publications, and has delivered over 1,000 lectures worldwide on his research.